BEHOLD YOUR GOD

MAGNIFY HIS MAJESTY

BEHOLD YOUR GOD: MAGNIFY HIS MAJESTY

Written by Frank Hamrick and Jeff Hedgepeth

Copyright © 1980, 1983, 2000, 2009 by Positive Action for Christ, Inc., P.O. Box 700, 502 West Pippen Street, Whitakers, NC 27891.

www.positiveaction.org

Fourth edition 2009
Third printing 2013

Printed in the United States of America

ISBN: 978-1-59557-108-3

Edited by Dennis Peterson, Kraig Keck, and C.J. Harris
Layout and Design by Shannon Brown
Artwork by Chris Ellison

Published by

Riley Martin

TABLE OF CONTENTS

PREFACE

The pastor strode to the New Park Street Chapel pulpit that Sunday morning, January 7, 1855, to deliver his sermon. His text was Malachi 3:6.

"The proper study of the Christian," he began, "is the Godhead. The highest science, the loftiest speculation, the mightiest philosophy, which can engage the attention of a child of God is the name, the nature, the person, the doings, and the existence of the great God which he calls his Father."

"There is something exceedingly improving to the mind in the contemplation of the Divinity," the pastor continued. "It is a subject so vast, that all our thoughts are lost in its immensity; so deep, that our pride is drowned in its infinity. Other subjects we can comprehend and grapple with; in them we feel a kind of self–contentment, and go on our way with the thought, 'Behold I am wise.' But when we come to this master science, finding that our plumb line cannot sound its depth, and that our eagle eye cannot see its height, we turn away with the thought, 'I am but of yesterday and know nothing.'"

The humble preacher who spoke those words was the "prince of preachers," Charles Haddon Spurgeon.

We know how he felt in addressing the fathomless topic of the Godhead. When the authors began the task of preparing this study, they, too, were nearly staggered by their feelings of awe and inadequacy. As their study progressed, those feelings not only persisted but also grew more acute.

For the Christian, and indeed for the whole world, the knowledge of God is essential. It is more important than the knowledge of anything—or everything—else. The greatest word in any language or dialect is *God*. The loftiest thought that the mind can entertain is the thought of God.

The prophet Hosea told the people that they were destroyed for a lack of knowledge of God (Hosea 4:6). This lack of knowledge of God results in a lack of spiritual life or power. Today, the world has little real knowledge of the one true God.

The authors offer this study as one opportunity for you to increase your knowledge of God. They pray that God will be honored through this material and that many "might know thee, the only true God" (John 17:3). Student, as you study this material, *Behold your God!*

How to Use This Book

This student textbook includes a number of unique features, including the following.

Introductory Reading Assignments

Every chapter begins with a brief introductory reading assignment that gives an overview of the lesson and helps you get an idea of what will be covered in that particular lesson. It provides a general blueprint by which the overall lesson will be built. These readings should prepare you for and be supplemental to the teacher's lecture and the accompanying notes that you should take during that time.

Notes from the Teacher's Lesson

Every chapter also includes charts and diagrams that your teacher will use in the class lectures. These charts provide the "tools" that will help you focus on the key points of the lesson. You should fill in the appropriate blanks as your teacher presents the lesson and study them for the quiz that follows the completion of each lesson. (The quizzes include material from both your textbook readings and the teacher's lesson.)

Student Work

Each lesson includes some work that you need to do at home. Normally you will want to do this work before your teacher begins teaching the lesson. That way you will have a pretty good understanding of the subject matter, which should make the class time more productive.

Application Activities

At the end of each chapter is a list of topics, project, and/or activities under the heading "Application Activities" that will help you make practical applications of the lessons you've learned. These activities are designed to be used at your teacher's discretion to help you develop, think about, and apply the principles learned from the introductory reading assignment and your teacher's lecture. They might be reading assignments, discussion or debate topics, review activities, or writing assignments. Your teacher may use all or only a few of these items as appropriate for your particular class and to fit the time available for your class.

Glossary

Although a study of theology (the doctrine of God) is rich in wisdom and knowledge for young people, the terms used are sometimes difficult to understand. Some of the expressions might seem obscure to you and their meanings difficult for you to understand. Therefore, your textbook includes a glossary of terms at the end. This feature should make it much easier for you to understand the terms used in this study. Look up any terms with which you are unfamiliar or the meanings of which you are uncertain. If a term is not in this glossary, look it up in a regular dictionary or a Bible dictionary.

A Word About Quizzes and Tests

Your teacher will evaluate your work using a variety of tools, including chapter quizzes, Scripture memorization, various activities and/or writing assignments, and possibly major tests covering several chapters, or units. The questions for the quizzes cover the material in both the student readings and the teacher's lecture notes. The quizzes are made up of a variety of types of questions, including matching, short answer, true–false, multiple choice, and essays. The unit tests cover from three to nine lessons, with the average number of lessons being about five. (Chapter 20 is a review chapter.) The same types of items will be used on the tests as are on the quizzes. The individual classroom teacher will determine various point values and grading scales.

UNIT 1

THE KNOWLEDGE OF GOD

"It is not what a man does that determines whether his work is sacred or secular, it is why he does it. The motive is everything."

—A. W. Tozer, *The Pursuit of God*

ISA 43:7

PHIL 3:10-11

COL 1:16

PS 19:1

IXΘΥΣ

LAYING THE FOUNDATION

"Glorifying God has respect to all the persons of the Trinity; it respects God the Father, who gave us life; God the Son, who lost His life for us; and God the Holy Ghost, who produces a new life in us…"

—Thomas Watson, *A Body of Divinity*

"Hello," the voice answered the telephone enthusiastically. "What is the purpose of your call?"

For a moment, the caller was silent, caught by surprise at the way the person on the other end of the line had answered. The caller needed help, but he'd never had someone ask him so bluntly what his purpose in calling was.

"Well, I, uh…I guess I'm not really…uh…sure why I'm calling," he stammered. "I…uh…heard that you were the 'On–Purpose Person,' and I sort of…well…thought you could help me."

Although the caller wasn't very articulate, he recognized that he was spending—rather, wasting—his life without a real purpose. He was seeking his purpose in life, trying to find meaning and thereby give his life significance. He wanted his life to count for something, but he just didn't know how to go about it.

Thomas Carlyle, a Scottish historian and philosopher of the nineteenth century, wrote, "The man without a purpose is like a ship without a rudder—a waif, a nothing, a no man. Have a purpose in life, and, having it, throw such strength of mind and muscle into your work as God has given you."

This advice is especially significant for a Christian teenager. God has a purpose, a will, for each of His children, and our responsibility is to discover that will and to fulfill it. "The man who succeeds above his fellows," Edward George Bulwer–Lytton wrote, "is the one who early in life clearly discerns his object and towards that object habitually directs his powers."

This opening chapter of your book and the teacher's lesson lay the foundation for this course by defining the ultimate purpose of every child of God regardless of age or any other distinguishing characteristic. That foundation principle is that man's chief end (primary purpose for being) is to glorify God in everything he does. To glorify God requires that we know Him personally and intimately. It is not sufficient to know merely *about* Him; we must know *God Himself.*

Keep this goal in mind as you proceed through this study. If you do, you will complete this course knowing not only your God–given purpose but also the God who gives that purpose.

Student Work

Nowhere does the Bible seek to prove God. His existence is assumed, and the Bible concludes, "The fool hath said in his heart, There is no God" (Ps. 14:1). Genesis opens with the simple words, "In the beginning God…." From that point, man is faced with one conclusion—*that God is.* From this conclusion we can draw from the rest of Scripture the following facts:

- God created all things
- God created all things for His own glory
- Man's chief end is to glorify his Creator

These three fundamental facts underlie all schools of learning and logic (e.g., philosophy, theology, sociology, science, and history). In fact, all knowledge rises or falls on an understanding and correct application of these premises. Therefore, we must begin this study by considering these three fundamental propositions.

Three Foundational Propositions

God Created All Things

Only three explanations can be given for the existence of all matter. These are summarized in the following table.

| Various Views of How Matter Came into Being ||
Explanation for the Existence of Matter	School of Thought
1. God created it.	Creationism
2. It evolved from nothing.	Atheistic evolutionism
3. God created the first matter and set in motion forces that caused it to evolve to its current state.	Theistic evolutionism

What is obviously wrong with the statement of atheistic evolutionism (i.e., that all matter evolved from nothing)? _____

_____

_____

_____

Because this theory is so obviously ridiculous and unscientific, most *honest* scientists have been forced to embrace theistic evolutionism.

Read 2 Peter 3:5. According to this verse, how did the earth come into being?_____

_____

How does God describe those who reject creationism?_____

_____

_____

God is saying, "Although scientists know they are wrong, they refuse to admit it!" Why will they purposefully reject a fact (creation) they know is true? Because to admit creation would be to admit the truth of our *second* foundational proposition, which follows.

God Created All Things for His Own Glory

According to Psalm 19:1, what do the heavens (sun, moon, stars, and planets) do? _____

_____

According to Romans 1:19–20, what do the things God has made cause men to understand? _____

_____

Why did God make all things (Prov. 16:4)? _____

Why were all things created (Col. 1:16)? _____

It is this singular fact that annoys scientists. If God made all things, then logic demands that all things—including man—are responsible to their Maker. In other words, if there is an Intelligent Maker of this universe and all that is in it, then the universe and everything (and everyone) in it belongs to Him, and He can do with it whatever He desires. This fact points to the third proposition, which follows.

Man's Chief End Is to Glorify His Creator

Isaiah 43:7 states…

how man came into being (_____

_____); and

why man was made (_____).

These facts disturb unsaved man. He wants to be his *own* master, responsible to no one but himself. To admit God is to admit that God has first claim on his life. Yet, all biblical and scientific facts thunder forth this far-reaching foundation principle. (Throughout this series of lessons, and especially in the final lesson, you will learn the "first-claim principle," that God has first claim on your life and every aspect of it. As you study each lesson, be looking for ways in which this principle is applicable.)

The Implications of These Propositions

Since man's chief end is the glorification of his Creator, we must ask ourselves how man glorifies God. Again, logic will answer our question. To glorify Him requires the following three things.

We Must Know Him

We cannot glorify one whom we do not know. What is God like? Who is He? What does He require of man? How does He think? What pleases Him?

One must know the answers to these questions if he is successfully to glorify God. Therefore, the primary goal of this study is to bring you to a personal knowledge of and relationship with God. We will study the Godhead (God the Father, God the Son, and God the Holy Spirit), not to learn facts *about* them, but to get to know them personally.

According to Philippians 3:10 and 14, what was Paul's primary goal? "[T]hat I _____…I press toward the _____ (goal) for the prize of the _____ _____ of God in Christ Jesus."

As we come to know Him, we find out how we can glorify Him.

We Must Be Holy

In Philippians 2:13–15, we learn God's will and pleasure for us (i.e., what God's will has determined will best please and bring glory to Himself). What is it, according to verse 15?_____
_____
_____
_____

Therefore, the second step toward glorifying God is to be blameless, or holy. During the teacher's lecture, listen for a definition of holiness, and write that definition in the following spaces: _____
_____
_____
_____

How do we see Philippians 2:13 in this definition? _____
_____
_____

Note the following two principles about holiness:

- God plans and accomplishes holiness in us; it is not something that we achieve by our own efforts.

- Holiness is first a matter of *being* and then a matter of *doing*.

We Must Walk Holy

First Peter 1:15 commands us to do what? _____
_____

(*conversation* meaning "conduct of life" or actions). Therefore, we are not only to *be* holy within but also to be holy outwardly. (In this study, we will call inward holiness *personal holiness*. We will call outward holiness *practical holiness*.)

Looking at Holiness

Study the following illustration for this concluding section of Lesson 1.

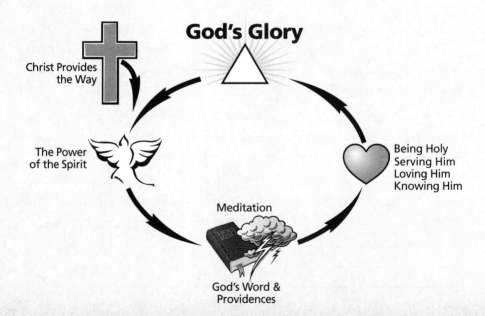

God the Father—Planner of Holiness

God the Father has planned our holiness, and it is to this end that we are saved. According to Ephesians 1:4, why are we saved? _____
_____
_____

God planned our holiness before He created the world! How does He state this in Ephesians 1:4?_____
_____
_____

Looking at the illustration, we see that God drew (diagrammed) the entire plan of our bringing glory to Him by *being holy* and *doing holiness*. Note the rest of God's plan in the following points.

Jesus Christ—Provider of Holiness

Christ came to earth to provide the means for our holiness. According to Titus 2:14, why did Christ come to earth?

To give _____ (His death on the cross)
To _____ (i.e., to free us on the cross)
To _____
_____ (i.e., make us holy)

Christ did not come to earth to save us from our sins! He came to make us holy! He died for our sins because that was necessary to accomplish His purpose. To say that Christ died only to save us from sin is to come short of God's real purpose of sending Christ. Therefore, man must be liberated from sin through the cross to be free for God to start him on the road to holiness.

Have you gone through the door of the cross? Have you been washed in the blood of Christ and redeemed (freed) from the curse of sin? If you haven't, trust Him now because God's plan requires everyone who brings Him glory to come by way of the cross. See your teacher today about your salvation.

Holy Spirit—Performer of Holiness

The Holy Spirit performs, or perfects, our holiness. Ezekiel 36:26–27, though speaking of Israel, is an example of what happens to a Christian when he trusts Christ. The Spirit enters him for what purpose?_____

_____

_____

_____

Thus, the Spirit comes into every believer and personally supplies him the power to be holy and to perform holiness. As we submit to Him, He does His work in us.

Challenge

Do you desire to bring glory to God? Do you long for a holy life? Would you like to know Him (not just know *about* Him but truly *know Him* personally)? Then study diligently with us in these lessons. Pray for God to make Himself more real to you this year. Memorize Philippians 3:10–11, and make it your prayer for the year:

> *That I may know Him,*
> *and the power of his resurrection,*
> *and the fellowship of His sufferings,*
> *being made conformable unto His death;*
> *if by any means I might attain unto the resurrection of the dead.*

Notes from the Teacher's Lesson

KNOW
(Mental acquisition of facts)

BE
(Personal holiness)

DO
(Practical holiness)

Holiness is the inward progressive work of the Holy Spirit through Christ of setting apart the believer from sin and to God.

The Father _____

_____

_____

_____.

Jesus Christ _____
_____. Christ died for us that He
might provide the way for us to be sanctified, set apart, made holy.

The Holy Spirit _____
_____.

Application Activities

1. Read and write a two–page summary of the principles contained
   in *The On–Purpose Person.* (Bibliographic data are given in the
   Recommended Reading List.)

2. Using eight sheets of paper, label each page with a different heading
   from the following list:

   • Physical/health/recreational
   • Financial/material
   • Family
   • Vocational/career
   • Social/community
   • Spiritual
   • Mental/educational/intellectual
   • Other

   On each sheet, list your wants, dreams, or goals for the appropriate
   headings. Study your list carefully. Then ask yourself the following
   question about each goal: "Can I pursue this goal to God's glory?" If
   not, strike it from your list. If you *can* glorify God through its pursuit,
   write a brief explanation of how you can best fulfill man's chief end in
   life by pursuing that goal and how it will bring glory to Him.

3. Read pages 6–26 of Thomas Watson's book *A Body of Divinity* (on
   man's chief end). List the four things of which he says that glorifying
   God consists and the seventeen ways he offers that we must glorify
   Him.

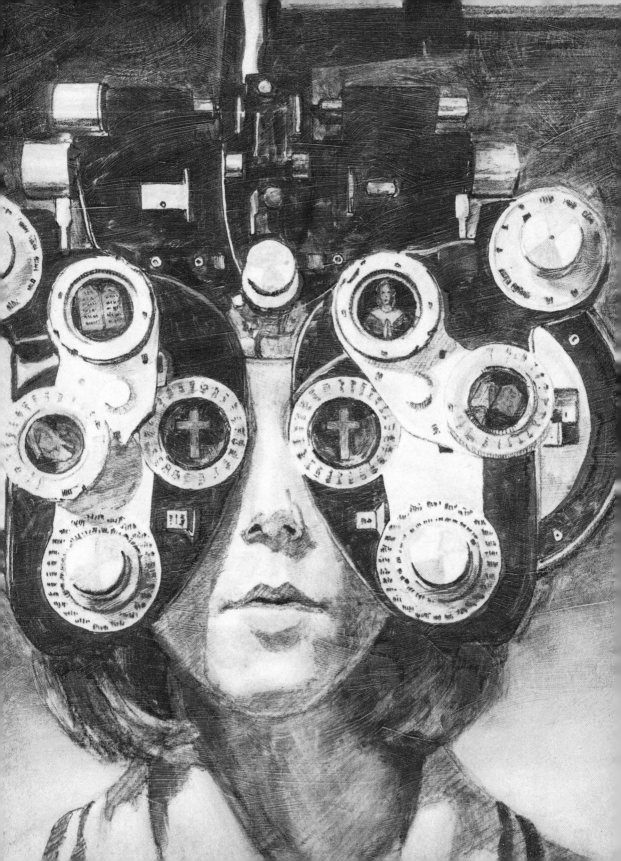

CHAPTER 2

GETTING A RIGHT FOCUS

"God must be the Terminus ad quem, the ultimate end of all actions."

—Thomas Watson, *A Body of Divinity*

Charlie Brown, artist Charles Schultz's born–loser cartoon character, thought he had found a sure–fire solution for success—at least in one small area of his dismal life. He took his bow, drew back the string with his arrow, aimed at the wooden fence across the yard, and released it. The arrow flew toward the fence and imbedded its head in the wood with a sharp WHACK! Then, as Lucy, his grumpy nemesis, watched, he raced to the fence and quickly drew a target around the still–quivering arrow.

"Hold it!" Lucy yelled. "That's not the way you do it! You're supposed to draw the target first and *then* shoot at it!"

"But my way guarantees success," Charlie Brown rationalized. "This way, I hit the target every time."

"Oh, good grief!" Lucy muttered as she walked away in disgust.

We chuckle at Charlie Brown's twisted logic, but we're often guilty of doing exactly what he did. In our pursuit as Christians of our ultimate goal, our chief end, in life—the glorification of God—we often focus on or aim at the fence rather than our real target.

This chapter and the teacher's lesson that goes with it will help you recognize how we often focus on the wrong things in our efforts to glorify God, thereby missing the mark. If we focus on the wrong things, the results will also be wrong. This chapter and the teacher's lesson, however, will help us adjust our focus so that we are emphasizing the right things in our lives and thereby accomplishing the right things and our chief end in life.

Notes from the Teacher's Lesson

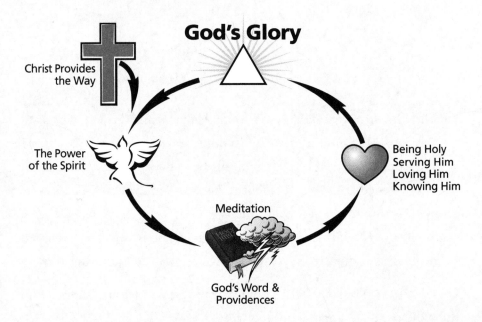

- The Christian's primary goal— _____
- The means to this goal— _____
- The primary focus of this goal— _____
  _____

The problem that occurs when one focuses on…
- holiness— _____
- the Word— _____
- love— _____
- rules and laws— _____

- doing— _____
- being— _____

The two components of love— _____

The things on which a Christian's focus should be when he reads and studies the Bible—_____
_____

Student Work

The Christian's Goal

As we have seen, God's ultimate goal for a Christian is His glorification through our being holy and practicing holiness. According to Ephesians 1:4, why has God chosen us? _____
_____

The Basis of the Goal

Love

Before one can be holy and practice holiness, he must love the Lord. Therefore, love is the *basis* of all holiness. How is this seen in Ephesians 1:4? _____
_____

The teacher's lesson used 1 Corinthians 13 as a further example of the fact that holiness is a by–product of love. As one loves the Lord (who is holy), he himself becomes holy. The same principle is often seen in married couples. Because of their love and fellowship with each other through the years, they gradually come to think, act, and sometimes even *look* alike!

We are commanded in 1 Peter 1:16, "Because it is written, _____ _____; for I am holy." In other words, if we concentrate our attention on the Holy One, we will become like Him. Thus, love for Christ produces holiness.

The Word

The life of David is an illustration of one who…
> studies the Word,
> sees the Lord, and
> falls in love with Him and thus
> seeks to be holy and
> seeks to serve Him.

This sequence is beautifully illustrated in Psalm 119, where we see the following progression.

His Goal

David's goal was the same as ours—holiness. How does verse 1 indicate this? _____

_____

_____

However, David knew better than to concentrate on being holy. To do that would lead him into what error (refer to the teacher's lesson)? _____

_____

_____ Thus, he quickly tells us the object of his focus or concentration in verses 1 and 10.

His Focus

What was David's focus (i.e., what did he seek)? _____

_____

What does that mean? _____

_____

_____

His Means

How was he to "see" the Lord? Verses 11, 15, and 16 suggest four ways he could see God. What phrase in each of these verses best fits each of the following means or methods?
- Memorizing the Word— _____

  _____

- Meditating on the Word— _____
  _____

- Enjoying the Word—_____
  _____

- Reviewing verses memorized— _____
  _____

The important thing to remember is that *it is not by studying the Word that we love God, but it is as we study God in the Word that we come to love Him.* According to the teacher's lesson, what sad result often accompanies studying the Word just for the sake of learning more about the Word (without seeking to learn of Him)? _____
_____
_____

Therefore, for what does David pray in Psalm 119:18? _____
_____
_____

What do you think these "wondrous things" were? _____
_____
_____

As God opened David's eyes to such things, what truth did David see about the Lord as recorded in each of the following verses?
- v. 27 – _____
- v. 41 – _____
- v. 52 – _____

His Love

David's seeing the Lord led him to love the Lord. How is this fact expressed in verse 57?_____
_____
_____

As he continued loving the Lord and seeing Him in the Word, David learned more of Him. What truth did he see in each of the following verses?

- v. 62 – _____
- v. 68 – _____

  _____
- v. 73 – _____

  _____
- v. 77 – _____
- v. 88 – _____

His Surrender

David's seeing God's love and falling in love with Him caused David to fall and confess the following:

- v. 94 – "I am _____."
- v. 125 – "I am thy _____."

Thus, we see the progression. We focus on Christ in the Word and thus learn to love Him. That love causes us to be holy and to serve the One we love.

Application Activities

1. Read the first verse of every Psalm and record on a separate sheet of paper all the things you learn about the Lord from each verse. (Not every first verse will speak directly of Him, but many of them will.)

2. Read and study about Paul's focus in Philippians 3:4–15. Then answer the following questions about the passage.
   - On what things had Paul been focusing before his salvation experience?
   - According to vv. 8 and 10, what became his focus after he was saved?
   - According to vv. 13–14, what was the ultimate goal toward which he was striving after his salvation?
   - What does he say concerning our focus in v. 15?

3. Jesus Christ's focus was to do "the will of the Father which hath sent me" (John 5:30). Study Christ's life and how He went about glorifying God. How did He respond in each of the following situations?
   - When He was angry
   - When He was in social settings
   - When He faced temptations
   - When He learned of others' misfortunes
   - When He learned of others' blessings
   - When He prayed

What can you learn from this about developing your own right focus?

Kings
Lion of Judah
Lord of Lords
Prince of Peace
Root of David
Saviour
Dayspring

CHAPTER 3

KNOWING GOD

"To glorify God is to have God–admiring thoughts, to esteem Him most excellent, and search for diamonds in this rock only."

—Thomas Watson, *A Body of Divinity*

"Me? Know God?" you might be asking. "But isn't God too big, too powerful, too complicated for *anyone* really to know?"

Certainly no one can ever know *everything* about God. But as A. W. Tozer wrote in *The Pursuit of God*, "Being made in His image [believers] have within [them] the capacity to know Him."

"Well, of course," you might say. "I realize that we can know Him in the sense that He has saved us, but can we *really* know Him—like, say, we know our friends at church or school?"

Yes. And Tozer continues, "We have almost forgotten that God is a Person and, as such, can be cultivated as any person can. It is inherent in personality to be able to know other personalities, but full knowledge of one personality by another cannot be achieved in one encounter." It requires repeated, long–term contact.

God is waiting for us to get to know Him. But we are so busy that we hardly come close to that goal. Oh, the things with which we're involved might be good things, but they tend to get our eyes focused on the wrong things rather than on God Himself.

How do you think a boy would feel if he took his girlfriend out to a nice, quiet restaurant where they could eat and talk, getting to know each other better, but the girl never paid any attention to him? Or if, rather than listening to him, she was watching other diners, studying their meals, eavesdropping on conversations at nearby tables, or watching traffic pass on the street outside? Do you think they would get better acquainted? Of course not. The boy would start looking for another girlfriend!

Similarly, Tozer said, "The simplicity which is in Christ is rarely found among us. In its stead are programs, methods, organizations and a world of nervous activities which occupy time and attention but can never satisfy the longing of the heart."

We learn much about God from His Word, but studying the Word alone is not sufficient, although many people stop at that. "The Bible is not an end in itself," Tozer wrote, "but a means to bring men to an intimate and satisfying knowledge of God, that they may enter into Him, that they may delight in His Presence, may taste and know the inner sweetness of the very God Himself in the core and center of their hearts."

That is the goal of this chapter—and of this entire course: that you may truly know God and delight in His presence. As you do so, you'll find that you will begin bringing your "total personality into conformity to His," and you will want to *continue* pursuing Him so you can know Him even better.

Notes from the Teacher's Lesson

Knowing God is *not*_____
_____
_____.

Knowing God *is*_____
_____.
_____

Student Work

Knowing God Involves a Personal Relationship

To know someone thoroughly requires a frequent and regular face–to–face relationship. Pen pals have written each other for years and have thus learned a lot *about* each other, but they could not say that they really *know each other* without meeting on a more personal basis. There must be *mutual* knowledge and acquaintance with each other to say that we really know a person.

As the last teacher's lesson pointed out, it is not only important that we know God but also that He knows us. Do you know God personally, and does He know you personally? That is the essential question.

According to Matthew 7:21–23, does everyone who says he knows the Lord truly know Him? _____ Is the power to perform miracles a sign that one knows God? _____ How do you know that these miracle workers did not know God? _____
_____

In other words, if God doesn't know us, then we can't know Him! The great question, then, is *Whom does God know?*

According to John 14:6, 9, 10, we come to know the Father through _____. Whom is it who knows the Father? _____
Who has seen the Father?_____
_____

Christ is the way to the Father. Only those who know Christ know the Father.

God Is Holy

The problems with knowing God are manifold. Besides being invisible and far beyond our human ability to understand, He is also holy. His holiness is best painted for us in 1 Timothy 6:15–16. Note the terrifying language of v. 16. Can man approach God by natural means? _____
God's holiness is so pure and bright that it would strike a person dead to walk into God's presence in his natural state.

Man Is Sinful

To complicate the matter further, man is by nature sinful. Sin is the very opposite of holiness; sin and holiness repel each other. A sinner could no more endure a moment in the burning presence of God than a piece of tissue paper could withstand a moment in a blazing furnace.

Christ Is the Mediator

Christ is man's bridge to a holy God. Note 1 Timothy 2:5. What is Christ called? _____Mediator_____ According to a dictionary, what does this word mean? _____
_____

Thus, according to 1 Timothy 2:6, Christ came to be a _ransom_ for us. That is, He came to pay the price for our sin, thereby making it possible (according to Col. 1:20–22) to _reconcile_ us to God by _____ so that those of us who were sometime _____ (separated) from God because of our sin could be presented to God _____, _____, and _____ in His sight.

Therefore, we see that *the only way a man can know God is to establish a personal relationship with Him through a personal acceptance (by faith) of Christ's offering Himself on the cross in payment of our sins.* (Note: Memorize this sentence!)

Knowing God Involves Personal Fellowship

We can approach God only through Christ, who is the Way (John 14:6), but knowing God as our Savior and Lord is only the first step in *really* knowing God. A person can be born into a family, but it will take years of personal fellowship within that family before the person can honestly say, "I *know* my family." A child may know who his father is and at two years of age may know a few things about his father, but if the father were to die at that point, the child would soon forget, and by the time the child was grown, he would say that he never really knew his father.

Therefore, you may have trusted Christ as Lord and Savior and can say that you know God in that way, but do you know Him as a grown child knows his father through a close, personal fellowship with Him?

We get to know the Father through the following personal dealings.

Through a Meaningful Prayer Life

Read Hebrews 10:19–22. What is the "the holiest" of which the writer talks about entering? _____

On what basis can a Christian enter boldly into this throne room of God? _____
(i.e., because he has accepted Christ as Savior and has a personal relationship with God).

A person who has not been washed in the blood has no grounds on which he can gain entrance into God's presence. Those who are born again, however, can go directly into God's presence. Therefore, we are here encouraged to draw _____ to God in prayer.

Read Hebrews 4:14–16. How does this passage say we can come to God in prayer? _____ As we go to Him in prayer, what do we obtain from Him? _____

_____

Thus, through prayer we get to know God more intimately. As He answers our prayers and as we unload our hearts to Him and receive relief, we learn more of His kindness and grace and tender mercies.

Are your prayers effective? Do you *enjoy* your prayer life? Do you realize that you are in God's presence when you pray? Do you harbor unconfessed sins that deny your admission into His presence? If so, deal with those sins by confessing them to Him immediately and thereby ensuring access to Him in prayer.

Through God–Centered Reading of the Bible

Earlier, we learned that it is not merely studying the Word but studying our *Lord* through the Word that draws us closer to Him. Through reading His Word we see His power, love, omniscience, faithfulness, and hundreds of other qualities and attributes of God. (We will examine each of these attributes in later lessons.)

Through Problems

Psalm 119:67–68 illustrates the goodness of God even in our problems.

- What was David's condition *before* he was afflicted?_____
_____

- What did his affliction cause him to do (v. 67)?_____
_____

- What, in turn, did the Scriptures do for him (you can assume this answer by reading his statement in v. 68)? _____
_____
_____
_____

Thus, David's problems were a blessing in disguise because they had caused him to see the hand of the Lord in his life. Here also is the importance of *recording in a notebook or journal* all of the things that God does for you in your life. This record will continually remind you and teach you of the goodness and glory of God.

Challenge

What about your *relationship* to the Lord? Have you come to God through the blood of Christ? If not, you can receive Christ as your Lord and Savior right now. Simply trust what He did for you on the cross as payment for your sins, repent of your sinful condition, and, recognizing that there is nothing you can do to save yourself, accept Christ's payment alone for your sins.

What about your *fellowship* with Him? Do you have an active, energetic, effective prayer life? Do you really "get in touch" with God in your prayers? If not, perhaps sins are standing between you and God. (David wrote in Psalm 66:18, "If I regard iniquity in my heart, the Lord will not hear me.") Confess those sins now, and restore your fellowship with the Father.

Do you have a right *attitude* when you read the Bible? Do you concentrate on learning of Him and letting Him speak to you through the Word? Do you study the Word with a view to fellowshipping literally with Him?

What about your problems? Do you record the way God uses problems and blessings in your life? *Do you really know Him?*

Application Activities

1. Read and report (either orally or in writing) on the lessons you learn about knowing God in A. W. Tozer's book *The Pursuit of God*. (Bibliographic data are in the Recommended Reading List.)

2. Defend with Scripture the following statement by Robert H. Benson: "There is but one thing in the world really worth pursuing—the knowledge of God."

3. A young pastor new to the village once visited philosopher Thomas Carlyle and asked him, "What do you think our church needs most?" Carlyle replied, "What this church needs is a man who knows God otherwise than by hearsay." Explain what Carlyle meant.

4. Write an essay explaining how one gets to know God through each of the following activities or circumstances:
   • Prayer
   • Bible reading
   • Listening to the preaching of the Word
   • The problems of life

5. How will a more intimate knowledge of God help you to focus on the right things and ultimately to glorify God?

shalt enlarge m

33 Teach me, O LORD, the way of th
statutes; and I shall keep it unto th
end.

34 Give me understanding, and
keep thy law; yea, I shall observe
my whole heart.

35 Make me to go in the path
commandments, for therein do I de

36 Incline my heart unto thy testi
ies, and not to covetousness.

37 Turn away mine eyes from
ing vanity; and quicken
way

38 Stablish thy word unto
who is devoted to thy fear.

39 Turn away my reproach
fear for thy judgments are goo

40 Behold I have longed aft
cepts: quicken me in thy rig

41 Let thy mercies come
O LORD even thy salvation

CHAPTER 4

INSTRUMENTS FOR KNOWING GOD: HIS WORD

"This blessed book will fill your head with knowledge, and your heart with grace."

—Thomas Watson, *A Body of Divinity*

It was originally planned as an Easter egg hunt for children ages twelve and under at the local farmers' market. But once the master of ceremonies announced the prizes, people of all ages suddenly joined the hunt.

"Inside each of these plastic eggs," his voice had crackled over the public address system, "is some kind of a prize. Most of them are filled with jellybeans. Others contain a solid chocolate egg. A small number of them even hold one–, five–, or ten–dollar bills."

One could hear the children, their parents, and even grandparents making excited exclamations to one another. The emcee had to quiet the crowd before he could continue with his explanation of the prizes.

"But the big surprise today is that inside *one* of these eggs—only *one* of them, mind you—is a *really* fantastic prize for whoever finds it."

The crowd waited expectantly in hushed silence.

"Inside one of these eggs is a certificate for *five hundred dollars!*

Now you know why formerly uninterested teenagers, adults, and senior citizens suddenly became little kids and joined in the egg hunt with gusto!

Christians have a prize that is worth far more than a mere five hundred dollars, yet amazingly few of them seem interested in searching for it. They'd rather devote their time and energies to striving for the transitory wood, hay, and stubble that the world offers.

That prize is enclosed in God's Word, the Bible. In it, God Almighty has spoken to us. "The two Testaments," Thomas Watson wrote, "are the two lips by which God has spoken to us." But we're often too busy or too distracted to hear Him. He has given this message to us as the instruction book for how we may fulfill our chief end of glorifying Him. In Watson's words, it is "a rule of faith, a canon to direct our lives. The Word is the judge of controversies, the rock of infallibility. It shows the *Credenda*, what we are to believe; and the *Agenda*, what we are to practice." If God "took pains to write, well may we take pains to read."

And how should we read it?

- We should read it with reverence.
- We should read it with seriousness.
- We should read it with affection.
- We should read it with love—as a love letter from God to us.

Dr. Walter Fremont, formerly professor of education and psychology at Bob Jones University, used to suggest that his students incorporate into their Bible reading exercises what he called the "Four–M Formula":

1. As you read an important Scripture truth, Mark it in your Bible.
2. Then Memorize it.
3. Throughout the day, Meditate on it.
4. And finally, by repeated applications of and thinking about the truth, you will Master it!

This chapter is designed to help you see—and act upon—the importance of reading and studying God's Word as a means of glorifying God.

Student Work

Review

Review your notes from the first three chapters, and then answer the following questions.

1. What is God's ultimate goal for each of His children? _____
   _____

2. To achieve this goal, what must we do and be? _____
   Thus, man's primary goal is personal holiness.

3. To achieve man's goal, he must have a correct focus. What is that
   focus? _____
   _____

4. What is the means of that focus? _____

5. State three reasons why, in light of the fact that God made us for
   His glory, we should be holy.

   • God the Father_____
     _____ .

   • Jesus Christ the Son _____
     _____ .

   • The Holy Spirit _____
     _____ .

6. Knowing God involves what two things?

   • A personal _____ with God
   • A personal _____ with God

7. Through what three personal dealings do we come to know God?

   • _____
   • _____
   • _____

Meditation

As we have seen, to know God one must focus upon Him in the Word of God. This lesson discusses the meaning of meditation on the Word.

Meditation is a lost art. During David's day (and even until recent times), men put much time into meditation, realizing the benefits of this daily exercise. As a result, men were deep in their love of and appreciation for the Lord. Their insight into God's Word was deep, and their writings drip with the honey of praise for the grace and glory of their God.

Meditation seems to have produced *dedication.* Conversely, one could easily conclude, a *lack of meditation produces spiritual stagnation.*

The Definition of Meditation

Meditation is a mental process through which one memorizes, visualizes, and personalizes Scripture. Through meditation, Scripture is taken through the mind, the will, and the emotions and results in greater love for the Lord and a life of holiness and faith.

The Focus of Meditation

Meditation focuses on the following two things:

- The Word of God
- God as revealed in His Word

Meditation, therefore, is much more than simply thinking about something. It is contemplating and concentrating on the Word of God with the purpose of getting to *know the God of the Scriptures.*

Note the focus or subject of David's meditation in the following verses from Psalm 119.

- v. 15 – _____
- v. 97 – _____
- v. 99 – _____
- v. 148 – _____

David's attention to the Word of God, however, was not an end in itself. According to Psalm 63:6, why did he delight in meditating on the Word of God? _____

_____

_____

According to Psalm 40:7, what is the purpose of the Scriptures? _____

_____—Therefore, to read the Scriptures and not focus on Christ is to miss the whole point of the Bible. David's delight in the Word was based on the fact that the Word_____

_____.

The Benefits of Meditation

David is not the only Bible character who knew the joys and blessings of meditation. Joshua was also a man of meditation. What did God promise Joshua in Joshua 1:8 if he meditated on the Word? _____

_____

What did God promise David in Psalm 1 if he meditated on the Word?

_____

_____

_____

According to Psalm 94:19, what blessing and benefit did David derive from meditation on the Word?_____

_____

Clearly, then, regular meditation on God's Word brings success, prosperity, and delight.

Blessings

The next two lessons discuss the benefits and blessings of memorizing and meditating on God's Word. During these two lessons, we will discover fifteen blessings derived from meditation. These blessings can be divided into five groups of three blessings each. The five groups are as follow:

- Physical/material blessings
- Mental blessings
- Emotional blessings
- Volitional blessings
- Spiritual blessings

Physical/Material Blessings

Read each of the following verses and place beside it the blessing promised to the one who meditates on the Word of God.

Proverbs 4:8— _____

Read vv. 7–8. Who/what is "her" in v. 8? _____

Wisdom comes from the Word of God. Therefore, how does one "exalt her"? _____

_____

_____

_____

God promises that He will promote a person who desires to "get ahead" in life if he meditates on His Word! Rather than concentrating on advancing ourselves, we must concentrate on advancing *God*. When we do so, He will advance us! What do the following passages say in this regard?

- Psalm 84:11— _____

  _____

- Psalm 75:6–7— _____

  _____

- Psalm 37:4— _____

  _____

Proverbs 4:8— _____

If one embraces (loves and clings to) "her" (wisdom), God will bring honor to him or her. This is a promise of God. One who meditates on the Word will never have to seek his own honor and prestige. Men will honor him and seek him out because of both his power with God and his holy life.

Psalm 1:1–3— _____

This point will be discussed in detail in the next teacher's lesson.

Mental Blessings

The teacher's lesson will illustrate the mental blessings that result from meditation in the account of Bill Gothard. Other men who had similar experiences could be cited. For example, John Bunyan, an uneducated tinker, became one of the greatest and most brilliant writers and preachers of England. His most famous book, _Pilgrim's Progress_, ranks as one of the finest pieces of literature ever written—yet, his _only_ education was his hours of meditation on the Word as he walked the fields near his home in Bedford, England.

Read the following verses, and note the mental blessings that come from meditation.

Romans 12:2— _____

- As we pass God's Word through our minds, emotions, and wills, we find that His Word begins to sharpen our thoughts. Our minds are "renewed." What is the phrase that precedes the command to be transformed "by the renewing of your mind"? _____ _____

- The world colors our thinking. Television, magazines, friends, and other students at school all tend to press us into their mold. Before long, we begin to think as the world thinks (which is exactly opposite of the way God thinks). How do we keep our minds sharp? How do we keep thinking correctly? By renewing our minds through meditation on God's Word.

Isaiah 55:8–9— _____

_____

- Here we see that God does not think as man thinks. In fact, whatever your natural inclination, it will probably be the opposite of what God would do. God doesn't react as man does. God doesn't see things as man sees them. His ways are not our ways.

- How can one learn to see things as God sees them? _____

_____

- God's Word is an expression of the way God thinks. Someone has said that the Bible is God's brain. If we can constantly run His thoughts through our minds, pretty soon we will begin to think as He thinks. This is why the great Puritan writers had such depth of knowledge and such beautiful ways of expressing themselves. They had so saturated their minds with His Word that they literally "thought Scripture." Thus, we need to "let this mind be in [us] which was also in Christ Jesus" (Phil. 2:5). We need the "mind of Christ" (1 Cor. 2:16).

Psalm 119:97–98— _____

- According to Psalm 119:130, what does God's Word do to one's mind when it enters? _____
David explains what *light* is in the phrase that follows. What is it?_____

- There is a difference between knowledge and understanding. One can know facts but not understand them. How many times does David refer to *understanding* in Psalm 119? _____
_____ When one understands Scripture, he has wisdom.

One cannot understand Scripture unless . . .

- *he is saved.* What does 1 Corinthians 2:14 say about this? _____

_____

Only as a man knows Christ can he understand Scripture, for then—and only then—does he have Christ's mind.

- *he sees God in everything he reads in the Bible.* One must look for God in every verse. This is the secret to studying the Bible and developing a personal relationship with God.

- When we go to God's Word this way, it becomes (according to Ps. 119:24) our _____ . Each verse gives us advice. Each verse reveals the perfect will of God. Each verse gives us perfect light and insight for every decision. If we truly know God's Word, we have a perfect guide for every situation, and *as long as we follow that guide, we will never make a wrong decision*!

- One other thought. When God's Word becomes your counselor, you will not have to depend on your youth pastor, pastor, or parents for advice. In fact, according to Psalm 119:99, you will have __ _____ if your teacher is not also saturated in the Word.

Notes from the Teacher's Lesson

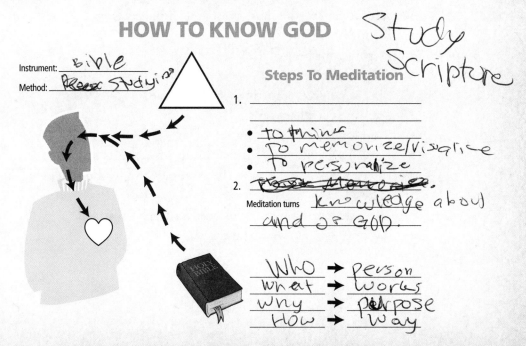

HOW TO KNOW GOD

Instrument: *Bible*
Method: *from Studying*

Study Scripture

Steps To Meditation

1. _____

- *to think*
- *To memorize/visualize*
- *to personalize*

2. ~~Read Memorize~~
Meditation turns *knowledge about* *and of GOD.*

Who	→	*person*
What	→	*works*
Why	→	*purpose*
How	→	*Way*

Application Activities

1. Read and meditate on Psalm 63:1–8. Record all of the things you learn from this passage as you truly meditate on it.

2. God's Word is not "just another book." It is special in many ways. Explain how it is special in the following ways:
   - Its antiquity
   - Its preservation
   - Its contents
   - Its prophecies
   - Its impartiality toward men
   - Its power and influence upon men
   - Its confirming miracles

3. Using a concordance, list the various similes and metaphors used to describe God's Word (e.g., Jer. 23:29 says that it is both a fire and a hammer).

3. Describe at least three methods of Bible study and how each of them can help you know God and His will better.

4. Explain the logic of each of the following ways compiled by Thomas Watson for getting the most from your Bible reading.
   - Remove hindrances.
   - Prepare your heart.
   - Read with reverence.
   - Persevere in remembering what you read.
   - Meditate on what you read.
   - Read it with an honest heart.
   - Pay as much attention to its commands as to its promises.
   - Pay particular attention to the examples and lives of the people in the Bible as living sermons.
   - Don't stop reading until you feel your heart warmed.
   - Put into practice what you read.

CHAPTER 5

INSTRUMENTS FOR KNOWING GOD: HIS PROVIDENCES

"...nothing comes to pass but what is ordained by God's decree, and ordered by His providence."

—Thomas Watson, *A Body of Divinity*

"How did you manage to escape from such a collision without a scratch?" the sports reporter asked the race car driver in a press conference following a fourteen–car pileup in which the racer's car hit the wall and flipped and rolled several times.

"I don't see how I did it," the driver answered, shaking his head in disbelief. "I just guess I was really lucky."

Luck, huh?

Was it also luck that caused a fellow driver to suffer a concussion, a broken arm, and several broken ribs?

"I guess it just wasn't his day. You know, we all go out there on the track not knowing if it's gonna be a good day for us, when Lady Luck smiles on us, or if it's a day when our number's up. We just never know."

This is what one regularly hears from the world as they try to explain the large and small events of life. Christians, however, should have a totally different explanation. It's called *the providence of God*, the manner in which God governs His entire creation. The very hairs of our heads are numbered (Matt. 10:30), and not a sparrow falls from the sky without God's knowledge (Matt. 10:29).

"There is no such thing as blind fate," Thomas Watson wrote, "but there is a providence that guides and governs the world." It "reaches to all places, persons, and occurrences." And it is always designed ultimately to result in God's glory.

Watson admonished his readers, "Learn quietly to submit to divine providence. Do not murmur at things that are ordered by divine wisdom. We may no more find fault with the works of providence than we may with the works of creation. It is a sin as much to quarrel with God's providence as to deny His providence."

In this chapter and the teacher's lesson, we focus on the role of providence as a means of knowing God.

Review

- What is the two–fold instrument by which a child of God gets truly to know his God? _____ _____

- What is the only method by which one can make this two–fold instrument effective in his or her life? _____ _____

- What are the two steps in this method? _____ _____ _____

- What are the three things one must do when exercising this method to turn knowledge *about* God into knowledge *of* God? _____ _____ _____

- What are the steps of the "Four–M Formula"? _____ _____

Notes from the Teacher's Lesson

In this lesson, we consider the second instrument by which we are able to focus on God—by meditating upon His providences. First, let's define *providences*, then we'll list four blessings of meditating on God's providences. Finally, we'll examine four steps involved in the exercise of meditation.

Definition of Providences

- _____
- _____
- _____
- _____

Four Blessings of Meditation

- _____
- _____
- _____
- _____

Four Steps of Meditation

1. _____
2. _____
3. _____
   - _____
   - _____
   - _____
   - _____
   - _____
4. The most important step:_____
   _____

Student Work

The Blessings of Meditation

In this lesson, we continue studying the fifteen benefits of meditation. The preceding lesson noted three physical/material benefits and three mental benefits. This lesson considers three emotional benefits and three volitional benefits.

Emotional Blessings

Read each of the following verses and place beside it the emotional blessing promised to the one who meditates on God in the Word and in providences.

Psalm 119:49; 94:19—_____

_____

- Notice Psalm 119:49 first. "Remember the Word unto thy servant" is David's way of saying, "Bring your Word to my mind so I can think about it." David was praying that God would help him think about (meditate on) Scripture. Why? Because he found _____ in the Word. This is a word akin to faith.

- Why does David "take heart" and increase his faith as he meditates? _____

  _____

  _____

  _____

- Meditation on God's Word—especially upon the great episodes in which God showed Himself mighty, faithful, and merciful to His children—is a great tonic for discouragement and sadness. Are things going against you? Meditate on what God has done in your life in the past, and then meditate on the providential care of God for His saints in the Scripture, and your spirits will rise to heights of joy.

Psalm 119:50, 52, 92— _____

_____

- Immediately after stating that God's Word was the source of his hope (v. 49), David adds that it is also his _____ _____. What did he do when he wanted to comfort himself (see v. 52)? _____

_____

_____

- That is, when David was discouraged, he reviewed all of the ways God had worked in men's lives in the past. When his enemies seemed to be prospering and gaining the upper hand, though they were wicked and he was godly, he reviewed God's past judgments against wicked men (such as the men in Noah's day who seemed to have the upper hand for 120 years while Noah was building the ark). Then he took heart, for he knew that eventually God would give him the victory and judge the sinner.

Psalm 119:28— _____

- The kind of strength to which David was referring is emotional. He had physical strength, but his spirit was sagging. Facing afflictions and enemies, he needed emotional strength. The practice of meditating on the Word and on the providences of God gave him the strength he needed to continue serving God.

Volitional Blessings

Volitional benefits are benefits that affect our wills. Remember, we take the Word, in meditation, through our minds, our emotions, and our wills. As it invades each of these areas of our souls, it has a distinct effect. Let's consider specifically three effects that meditation on the providences and the Word of God has on our wills.

Psalm 119:45— _____

_____

- Sin controls us; we don't control it. Occasionally, a Christian will be heard to say, "I can quit this sin any time I get ready." This boast assumes that we control sin. However, a careful study of the Word of

God reveals the opposite. What does John 8:34 say about this? _
_____

- Note Psalm 101:3. What does the last phrase of the verse indicate concerning "wicked things" and the "work of them that turn aside"? _____
_____

- We don't cling to sin; it hangs onto us like an octopus wrapping its arms around its victim. How does one break this awful death–hug? The key is in the first phrase of the verse, which says what?
_____
_____

- How does this keep sin from clinging to us? _____
_____
_____
_____

- A person who occupies his mind with the world (through television, movies, ungodly books, rock music, etc.) becomes a servant to sin. He loses his willpower, and though he may beg to be released and try a hundred different ways to "reform" or quit his sin, he finds himself helpless to do so. His will has become enslaved by sin.

- Now we come to Psalm 119:45. According to this verse, how does one free himself from the grip of sin?_____
_____

- As a person occupies his mind and fills his thoughts with God's Word and providences, the hold of sin on him will gradually weaken and finally fall off, freeing his will to once more choose that which is right.

Psalm 119:133; 40:8—_____

- Every Christian wants to know God's will. Yet, God has already revealed His will. According to these verses, where has He revealed His will?_____

- Michael Boland, in his preface to John Flavel's book *The Mystery of Providence*, states, "…in an ultimate sense, we can never be 'outside of the will of God.' Flavel would teach us that God's will for us is our duty to be found in His Word."

- That's a powerful statement! What does he mean, we can never be outside of the will of God? Notice that he said "in the ultimate sense." That is, God has a design for you, and He will not fail to accomplish that design. We might fight against His will, but we are only destroying the joy and blessings He has designed for us when we do so. Instead, we should be found studying the Word and meditating upon Him in the Word. Thereby we will walk in accordance with His will and enjoy all of the benefits as well. (We will have our cake and eat it, too!)

Psalm 119:73— _____

- It is one thing to *know* God's will; it is quite another thing to *do* His will. Where do we get the power to do what God bids? Through meditation! This is why so many of us fail—we don't meditate.

- How many times have you committed yourself to be a better witness? How many times have you given up a sin and confessed it to God only to go right back to it? How many times have you said, "I want to live for God, but I just can't seem to do it?"

- Now you know why! You have a will that is bound by sin. That will can be freed only by pondering regularly the things of God.

Challenge

Consider carefully the following words of John Flavel.

"O, is your life such a continued throng, such a mad hurry that there is no time for Christians to sit alone and think on these things, and press these marvelous manifestations of God in His providences upon their own hearts?

"I cannot but judge it the concern of Christians that have time and ability for such a work, to keep written memorials or journals of Providence by them…. Some say the art of medicine was acquired and perfected thus.

"If Christians in reading the Scriptures would judiciously collect and record the providences they shall meet with there, and (if destitute of other helps) but add those that have fallen out in their own time and experience, O what precious treasure would these make! What an antidote would it be to their souls against the spreading atheism of these days, and satisfy them beyond what many other arguments can do, that 'The Lord, he is the God; the Lord, he is the God' (1 Kings 18:39).

"Do not trust your slippery memories with such a multitude of remarkable passages of Providence as you have, and shall meet with in your way to heaven.

"Take heed of clasping up those rich treasures in a book, and thinking it enough to have noted them there; but have frequent recourse to them, as oft as new needs, fears or difficulties arise and assault you…. Make it as much your business to preserve the sense and value as the memory of former providences, and the fruit will be sweet to you."

Application Activities

1. For one week (or one month), keep a "Providence Journal" in which you record the various providences of God in your daily life.

2. List and explain examples of God's providence at work in American (or world) history.

3. Explain the following statement in the light of God's providence: "For the believer, there are no accidents."

4. Read and summarize the main points learned in William S. Plummer's book *Jehovah–Jireh: A Treatise on Providence.*

CHAPTER 6

THE MAN WHO KNOWS GOD: HIS PRIORITIES

"Aim purely at God's glory. We do this when we prefer God's glory above all other things; above credit, estate, relations; when the glory of God coming in competition with them, we prefer His glory before them."

—Thomas Watson, *A Body of Divinity*

We're all busy, whether we're students, parents, businessmen, or pastors or teachers. Those who are truly successful, however, are so because they have learned to establish priorities, ranking all of the many things they must do according to their relative importance in the overall scheme of things. Successful people see the "big picture" and set goals whereby they can achieve their priority tasks. They do not allow themselves to get buried under the avalanche of myriad activities of lesser importance.

"The secret of success," achievement experts Denis Waitley and Reni Witt state, "is *setting priorities.*"

Most of us just have too many irons in the fire at once. We are so busy trying to do too many things, thereby ensuring that we do nothing really well. Efficiency expert Thomas J. Peters wrote, "If you're…working 25 priorities, you don't have *any* priorities." The problem with many people who are climbing the ladder of success is that when they finally get to the top, they discover that they've had their ladders leaning against the wrong wall. They've set the wrong priorities. They've chased a vague idea of "happiness," or wealth or worldly "success." But these things, Waitley and Witt declared, "are *by–products*…they cannot be the goals themselves."

Establishing a few God–honoring priorities involves two related activities: *efficiency*, or doing things right, and *effectiveness*, which is doing the right things. As our priorities are established, we can focus on doing those few things well.

So far in this study, we've learned that man's primary God–given purpose for being is to glorify Him in all things. That "chief end" becomes the centralizing point of all our thoughts and actions. It helps us determine all of our other priorities in life. And those priorities guide our decisions when our duties seem to conflict and to compete for our limited time and energy.

Baseball player–turned–evangelist Billy Sunday said, "The man who tries to do a thousand things never will get anywhere. A jack of all trades never stands a chance." (The phrase *a jack of all trades and a master of none* is actually a perversion of the original saying: "a jack of all trades and a master of *one*.)

Don't try to be what you are not or what God doesn't intend you to be. Rather, find out what you are, what He wants you to be—and then be your best at it.

And set your goals and standards high. As Leonard Read wrote, "High aims form high characters." The goals and priorities you set begin your thoughts and behavior, and those determine consequences, whether for good or ill. No one who is content pursuing purely temporal goals and priorities will ever achieve eternal gains. The Christian should, in the words of Dr. Bob Jones, Jr., "Get a vision as broad as the needs of men and as deep as the love of God." That—and only that—will lead to a life that glorifies God in all of its parts.

This chapter and the teacher's lesson are aimed at helping you establish God–honoring priorities.

Review

State how each of the following goals is achieved.

- A Christian brings glory to God by _____ _____ .

- A Christian becomes holy by _____ .

- A Christian turns knowledge *about* God into knowledge *of* God by _____ _____ .

- A Christian comes to know God by _____ _____ .

- A Christian comes to love God by _____ .

- Meditation in the Word and in the providences of God causes one to know God by _____ _____ .

What are the four steps required in meditating on God in His providences?

- _____
- _____
- _____ _____
- _____

What are the five things one must ponder when meditating on God in His providences?

- _____ _____
- _____ _____
- _____
- _____
- _____

Notes from the Teacher's Lesson

THE MAN WHO KNOWS GOD: HIS PRIORITIES

Mankind's Greatest Need: _____

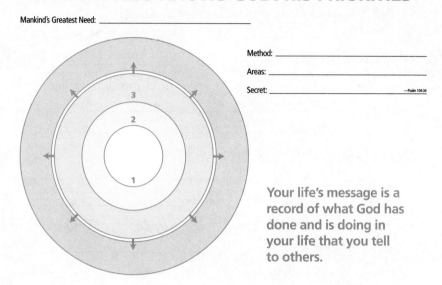

Method: _____

Areas: _____

Secret: _____ —Psalm 104:34

Your life's message is a record of what God has done and is doing in your life that you tell to others.

Student Work

Spiritual Blessings of Meditation

This lesson addressed the three spiritual benefits of meditation, thus concluding the fifteen benefits of memorizing and meditating on the Lord through the Word of God and providences.

Psalm 17:4; 119:9, 11— _____

_____

According to these verses, if one meditates on the Word, he will find that God will bring back to his mind the exact verse needed when he is faced with one of the following problems:

- A temptation to sin
- A difficult situation or circumstance
- A difficult decision

Accordingly, one should memorize and meditate on three types of verses for these three types of needs. Consider, for example, the following table.

Types of Verses for Memorization and Meditation	
The Need	**Subject for Memorization and Meditation**
Temptation to sin	Passages or providences that deal with temptations to sin. These are called weapons because they can be used as a weapon against temptation to sin.
Difficult situations	Promises in the Word or providences you have recorded that show how God took care of you or someone else in a similar situation or circumstance.
Difficult decisions	Principles that show how God works and thinks.

If you do not have some plan of meditation, you are leaving yourself defenseless against the onslaughts of Satan.

Note the following illustration. When you have wrong thoughts (or face a tough situation or decision):

- Turn it into a discussion with God.
- Expose the problem to the Scriptures (find a verse if you do not already have one).
- Claim specific principles and promises of God's Word.
- Record the type of thought, the verses used, and the results for future reminders.

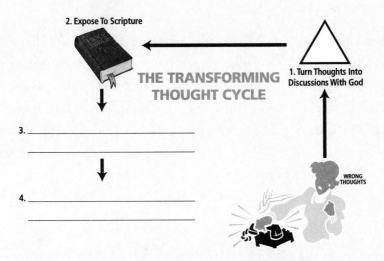

2. Expose To Scripture

THE TRANSFORMING THOUGHT CYCLE

1. Turn Thoughts Into Discussions With God

WRONG THOUGHTS

3. _____

_____

4. _____

_____

Hebrews 4:12—

Here we see that one who meditates on the Word sees himself as he really is. There is no way that a child of God can focus on the Word without seeing how ungodly he is in contrast to our glorious God.

Psalm 119:36— _____

Covetousness simply means "wanting things." It describes living to own and enjoy things. How often do we find ourselves in this position? The way to avoid covetousness is to wrap your mind around this verse and get your mind back on the things of the Lord when you start wanting things.

Application Activities

Beginning with this lesson, you will complete two projects each week. First, you will read an assigned chapter in the Bible and record all of the things you see about God as you meditate on the chapter. Second, you will meditate on the Lord in His works (providences).

Project One

1. Read Psalm 105 and record the characteristics of God that you see in this chapter. This psalm records Israel's history, highlighting God's wondrous works. It begins by calling on God's people to *remember* His providences (vv. 1–6), then it continues by calling attention to God's goodness in His covenant with Abraham (vv. 8–15), the lives of Joseph and Israel in Egypt (vv. 16–24), and in the life of Moses (vv. 25–38), and His care for them in the wilderness (vv. 39–41) and in their entering of Canaan (vv. 42–45).

    After carefully recording the things you learn about the Lord in this chapter, give the sheet to your teacher.

Project Two

2. Each week, your teacher will assign you one of four categories in which you are to meditate upon the providences of God. Following are the categories and an explanation of each.

- Bible characters—Different characters from the Bible will be assigned during the year. You will ponder the life of the one assigned and record the things you learn about God from the person's life.
- Historical events—You will be assigned an event in history, and you are to meditate on the providence of God evident in the event.
- Contemporaries' experiences—Contemporaries include friends and family members. You will record in this category the things that happen to those who reveal the Lord.
- Personal incidents—Here you record the providences of God that you experience firsthand in your own life.

Record the following things for the assigned category.
- Date and situation – Describe the particular event you are analyzing. (Example 1: "August 12, 20—. I was delayed leaving on a trip for three minutes by a telephone call from my aunt. As a result, I missed being on a bridge that collapsed with eighty–four people injured.") (Example 2: "September 21, 20—. I was saved while in the hospital with a back injury sustained from a fall off a pier at the beach.")
- What God did – State what you believe God did at that moment. (Example: "He had my aunt call me" or "He allowed my fall so I would be in a position to think, and then He sent my Sunday school teacher to visit me.")
- Timing – Timing is not always involved, but when it is, state how it figured into the providence. (Example: "If my aunt had called me one minute later, I would have been out of the house and involved in the bridge collapse.")
- Leading providence – Describe one event that led to another. (Bible example: Jesse sent David to carry provisions to his

brothers. While this task seemed unimportant at the time, it led to David's being at the right place to fight Goliath.) Such events are called the "leading edge" of a greater providence of God. They reveal God at work in the "insignificant" things. (Another example: Because your boss fired you, you were free to go to camp, where you were saved.)

- Instrument—A person (stranger, enemy, or friend) or thing that God uses to perform His providence. (Examples: Your aunt, your boss, a flat tire, etc.)

- Scripture fulfilled—Usually some Scripture (a promise, weapon, warning, or command) will be perfectly illustrated or proven true by your experience.

- Character of God—Record every aspect of the character of God you see revealed in the incident. (Examples: His sovereignty, mercy, compassion, omnipotence, loving kindness, goodness, omniscience, etc.) Then state *how* you saw these characteristics.

- What if…?—Cite as many "what if…" situations as come to your mind. (Examples: What if my aunt had not called? What if I had left the house earlier? What if I had not been fired? What if I had not had a flat tire?) As you cite these hypothetical situations, you will find that you will further see the hand of God at work in every detail of your life.

3. Trial assignment: Take an example from the first five years of your life. Category: Personal. (Hint: Talk to your parents about things that happened that you don't remember. Perhaps you can even record something that revealed the hand of God even at your birth.)

4. Refer to Application Activity No. 2 at the end of Chapter 1. Review the goals you wrote down for each of the eight categories in that activity. After reading Chapter 6 and listening to the teacher's lesson, do you need to revise any of your goals or add new goals? Do all of your goals honor and glorify God? Make any necessary additions, adjustments, or revisions. Then determine steps by which you can achieve each of these goals. Where possible, set a deadline for achieving each goal. Then begin *today* to make those goals completed tasks.

5. List the names of people whom you consider to be successful at setting godly priorities. Interview several of these people about how they arrived at their priorities and the advice they would offer to young people who want to honor God. Report—either orally or in writing—on what you learn.

6. Purchase (or make on your computer) a week–at–a–glance calendar. Write your deadlines for your annual, monthly, and weekly goals on this calendar. Make weekly and daily "to–do" lists. Begin working *today* to make your long–range goals completed tasks. Check off each item as you finish it.

7. When you die, for what would you most want to be remembered? (Or, what message do you want your life to leave behind for others to see?) Under the following categories, list the things for which you would want people to remember you:
   • General accomplishments
   • Character traits
   • Spiritual qualities
   • Academic achievements
   • Family life

   Then write out the steps you can take *today* to make each of those desired memories a reality.

CHAPTER 7

THE MAN WHO KNOWS GOD: HIS CHARACTERISTICS

"Though the main work of religion lies in the heart, yet our light must so shine that others may behold it. The safety of a building is the foundation, but the glory of it is in the frontispiece; so the beauty of faith is in the conversation."

—Thomas Watson, *A Body of Divinity*

Successful people in every profession possess certain qualities or characteristics that have made them successful. For example, for a professional athlete those characteristics include physical strength, stamina, speed, quickness, patience, good reflexes, self–discipline, mental alertness, and excellent hand–eye coordination. A successful businessman must have knowledge of his customers, his competitors, and his products or services; good financial skills; and an ability to plan for the future, anticipating problems or trends before they arise. And a good manager or administrator must have excellent decision–making skills.

It's no different for successful Christian living. If one truly wants to glorify God in his or her entire life, he or she must possess certain qualities or characteristics that will ensure a life–changing, life–influencing knowledge of God.

One's knowledge of God must go beyond mere profession; it must— and will—be seen in outward actions, behavior, and conversation. (The Elizabethan English word used in the King James Version of the Bible for such conduct, *conversation*, includes *all* outward behavior, not just spoken words.) How well you know God is evidenced by how you live your life daily.

Major League pitcher Orel Hershiser once told of meeting the late Frank Sinatra, who gave him an autographed photo of himself. Sinatra signed it, "To my great friends, *Oral* and Jane." His misspelling of Hershiser's first name showed how close these "friends" *really* were!

Student Work

The teacher's lesson for this chapter discusses four broad characteristics of the man who knows God. Those four characteristics include many of the more specific qualities that R. A. Torrey discussed in his book *How to Succeed in the Christian Life*. Some of them are as follows:

- Open confession of Christ
- Assurance of salvation
- Church membership
- Regular and consistent Bible study
- Active service for Christ
- The wise choice of companions

The "Application Activities" section of this chapter and the Recommended Reading List include other books that will be of great benefit to you as you seek to develop these essential characteristics and thereby bring glory to God through your life.

Read Colossians 1:28. What goal does this verse set for a Christian? ____
_____
_____

Read James 1:2–4 and 1 Peter 2:20–23. What do these passages teach concerning the Christian and suffering? _____
_____
_____
_____
_____

Read Romans 5:3–5. What sequence of growth is outlined in this passage?

_____

_____

_____

_____

_____

Review

List *in order* the three priorities of the man who knows God.

- _____

  _____

- _____

- _____

Which is our responsibility and which is God's responsibility: one's family, one's ministry? _____

_____

By what method do we deepen our relationship with the Lord?_____

_____

In what two things are we to meditate? _____

and_____

What is the secret of meditation? _____

What is a life message? _____

_____

_____

Notes from the Teacher's Lesson

THE MAN WHO KNOWS GOD: HIS CHARACTERISTICS
PSALM 1:1-3

Separated (v. 1)

Studious (v. 2)

Steadfast (v. 3)

Priorities

1. _____

2. _____

3. _____

Successful (v. 3)

Requirements

_____ _____> _____ _____   _____ _____

Application Activities

1. Meditate on the Lord as revealed in Psalm 103. Record all of the things you see about Him in this chapter. Continue meditating on the providences of God in the life of a contemporary (something they can share with you that happened to them in the last five years). A contemporary is any person now living.

2. Read and report—either orally or in writing—on one of the following books (bibliographic data for each book are in the Recommended Reading List):
   - *How to Succeed in the Christian Life* by R. A. Torrey
   - *The Christian's Secret of a Happy Life* by Hannah Whitall Smith
   - *Biblical Separation* by Ernest Pickering
   - *Spiritual Intimacy* by Richard Mayhue
   - *The Power of Commitment* by Jerry White

3. Make two lists, one of characteristics of spiritual *maturity* and another of characteristics of spiritual *immaturity*. Rate yourself—on a scale of one to ten, with one being least mature and ten being most mature—on each of those characteristics.

UNIT 2
THE NATURE OF GOD

"No man doth exactly know himself, much less doth he understand the full nature of a spirit; much less still the nature and perfection of God."

—Stephen Charnock, *The Existence and Attributes of God*

CHAPTER 8

A SPIRIT AND A PERSON

"God is a Spirit…He gave us a spirit with one object of holding fellowship with Himself."

—Andrew Murray, *God's Best Secrets*

Roger was excited as he entered his work station. When he came into the building, Jason, a friend and coworker, informed him that Mr. Gerschwin, the owner of the company, was going to visit their office that day. Roger had been in his job with the company only a few weeks, but he had already heard a lot about the owner. Some of what he had heard had been bad and disturbed him. But other comments had been good, offering him encouragement.

When he learned that the owner would be visiting the office that day, he was both excited and somewhat apprehensive. What was the owner *really* like? Was he stodgy, aristocratic, hard–nosed, and demanding? Or was he fair, affable, and understanding of his employees and their challenges?

As the morning hours passed slowly, Roger kept looking over the wall of his workstation at every sound of voices, wondering if they signaled the arrival of the owner. But he was always disappointed. He could hardly get any work done for thinking about meeting his boss, but he finally lost himself in his pile of paperwork.

"Excuse me, sir." An unfamiliar voice drew Roger from his reading. "Could you tell me where I could find Roger Scherer?"

"I'm Roger," he said tentatively to the stranger. "May I help you?"

"Oh, hi, Roger. I'm John Gerschwin. I heard you were one of our newest employees, and I just wanted to stop in and introduce myself. How is the job going so far?"

Roger's tongue was tied momentarily. He stumbled on the leg of his chair as he hurried to shake the owner's hand. He finally managed to stammer, "I'm glad to meet you, sir. The job's going fine."

"I hope you're learning a lot," Gerschwin said.

"Oh, yes, sir!" Roger fidgeted nervously. He noticed that in his haste to greet the owner he had knocked a stack of papers onto the floor. He wanted to pick them up, but he didn't want to interrupt the owner or appear to be inattentive to him. Gerschwin noticed Roger's discomfort.

"Here, let me help you with those papers," he offered, stooping to retrieve a file folder that had landed at his feet. As he bent, so did Roger. Their heads banged together with a thud. Roger blushed beet red.

"We're not getting off to such a great start, are we?" laughed Gerschwin. He quickly retrieved the papers and stacked them in Roger's trembling arms. "Say, it's nearly lunch time. Why don't you be my guest at lunch? That'll give us a chance to get to know one another better. Just don't spill your coffee on me!"

Roger accepted the invitation with misgivings, fearing that he would make an even greater fool of himself and alienate his boss even more. But the meal went extremely well, and he got to know more about his boss. He learned that he was a normal person just like himself. And he learned that Mr. Gerschwin was, indeed, a stickler for details and demanded a lot of his employees. But he also learned that Mr. Gerschwin had a sense of humor, was compassionate and understanding, and was willing to do anything he could to make his employees successful in their jobs.

Roger returned to his workstation with a greater respect for his boss and a determination to work hard to please his boss. Learning firsthand what Mr. Gerschwin was like made a world of difference in how he viewed his work for the company. As he went home that night, he thought about how his experience that day was similar to one's impressions about God. If one has misconceptions about God, they color how he reacts to and serves God. Once he really gets to know the Lord, however, it makes a world of difference in both his outlook on the spiritual life and the way he serves the Lord.

Student Work

What comes to our minds when we think about God is the most important thing about us.

A.W. Tozer stated, "The history of mankind will probably show that no people has ever risen above its religion, and man's spiritual history will positively demonstrate that no religion has ever been greater than its idea of God."

The most revealing thing about a nation, an individual, or a church is its conception of God. Someone has said, "Theology determines methodology." That is, what one thinks about God will determine:

- How he acts
- What methods he will use to serve God
- What attitude he will have

It is absolutely imperative, then, that we have a proper conception of God as He really is.

What is God like? We might answer that question by saying that God is not like anything; that is, He is not *exactly* like anything or anybody. That is the glory of God—there is nothing to which we can compare Him exactly! Note that in Scripture the prophets who tried to describe God made ample use of the word *like*.

For example, read Ezekiel 1:4–14. How many times did Ezekiel use the following words in his description of God?

- *like*—_____
- *likeness* —_____
- *appearance* —_____

Ezekiel saw heaven opened, and he found himself looking at that which he had no language to describe. The nearer he approached the throne of God, the less sure his words became. In 1:26–28, he sees the glory of God Himself. Note how many times he uses the following words or phrases to describe the scene:

- *likeness*—_____
- *appearance*—_____
- *as it were* —_____

Note that Ezekiel, in describing God, takes that which is *not* God and uses it to help us visualize what He *is* like. Thus, whatever we visualize God to be, He is not; for we have constructed our conception out of that which is not God. To understand God as He really is is not possible on this earth. However, to understand Him as He has revealed Himself in His Word and in providences is our greatest duty, our most important task.

Why We Must Know What God Is Like

Salvation Depends upon a Proper Conception of God

Unless a man sees God as holy and understands something of that holiness, he will not see himself as a sinner (or he will not see his sin as it really is) and therefore will not come to see his need of trusting Christ.

Read Isaiah 6. What brought Isaiah to declare himself a sinner? _____
_____
_____

Idolatry Feeds upon a Misconception of God

Idolatry is putting other things (e.g., sports, girls, boys, hobbies, clothes, cars, jobs, homes, or money) before God. Why would we put any of these things before God? Because we lose sight of who God is and what He is like!

Romans 1:21–23 gives a good example of this. What sin did they commit concerning God in verse 21? _____
_____That sin led to

what other sin in verse 23? _____

_____

_____

Service Rests upon Our Conception of God

After Isaiah saw God's holiness, what did he say in Isaiah 6:8? _____

_____

When one sees God in all of His glory, beauty, majesty, and power, he is then ready to serve Him. The root problem of people who are lazy in serving God, unfaithful in church attendance, stingy in giving of their income, and who live as they please is a misconception of God.

All Doctrine Is Based upon Our Conception of God

God is the Source of all things, including doctrine. We view God's doctrines according to how we view Him. For example, people who see God as a God of love and not of wrath conclude that there is no hell. People who see God as merely an impersonal force are susceptible to believing in theistic evolution. In turn, those who believe in theistic evolution see no miracles in the Bible and therefore rule out the miracle of the new birth.

God Is a Spirit

John 4:19–24 describes God as a spirit. How does Colossians 1:15 describe Him? _____

What information does Luke 24:39 add to this? _____

_____

_____

Does this imply that He doesn't have a body? _____

What does 1 Corinthians 15:44 say about this subject? _____

_____

_____

The basic difference between spiritual and earthly bodies seems to be in their composition, as the following table shows.

Natural Bodies and Spiritual Bodies Contrasted	
Natural Body	Spiritual Body
Temporal	Eternal
Visible	Invisible
Can be in only one place at a time	Is everywhere at once
Cannot "flow through" matter	Is not limited or bound by matter

What example of the last point in the preceding table do we see in John 20:19? _____

_____

_____

From this understanding of God we can see why images are wrong. According to Isaiah 40:25, why are images wrong? _____

_____

_____

Application

According to John 4:19–24, how is God to be worshipped? _____

_____

Since God is a spirit, He can be worshipped only in spirit. But what is spirit? In Hebrews 4:12, you will note that man is composed of the following three parts:

- Body ("joints and marrow")
- Soul
- Spirit.

Note also 1 Thessalonians 5:23. What parts of man are mentioned in this verse? _____

Let's define each part.

- Body—the material, physical aspect of our body that puts us in touch with the physical world about us through our senses
- Soul—our emotions, the seat of our personality
- Spirit—our innermost being, our means of communication with God

When God created man, He made him "in His image." As God was the "three–in–one" (Father, Son, and Holy Spirit), so He made man with a body, a soul, and a spirit. Through man's spirit God communicated with Adam. However, Adam fell into sin, and God, being a holy God, had to break His communication with man. Thus, man's spirit was "cut off" from God.

What words do Ephesians 2:12 and 4:18 use to describe this "cutting off" from God? _____

_____

_____

_____

Note: the word *alienated* means "to cut off." Man operated as a two–part being with the spirit lying dormant and inoperable. It is this restlessness and unsuccessful effort of the spirit of man to find its resting place in God that causes men to run from one fad to another, to turn to drinking and drugs, and to commit horrible crimes. Man's spirit is not satisfied with such things, for it was made to function only in connection with God.

Therefore, God sent Christ to remove the sin that blocks man's spirit from uniting with God. Through His blood, He paid for our sins, and all who accept His payment by placing their faith and trust in Christ are "made whole" and are once more reunited with God. Thus, the spirit part of man is "quickened" (made alive) by faith in Christ and once more has the privilege of operating the way it was originally created to operate—in God.

In the following diagram, we see man's spirit as his innermost being, his soul as comprising three parts (mind, will, and emotions), and his outward body.

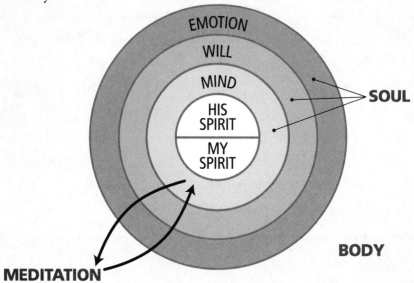

True worship is to occur in the spirit. But how is this done? To worship Him in spirit requires the following three conditions.

One's Spirit Must Be Made Alive in Christ

Thus, a lost man cannot worship God, for his spirit is severed from God.

One's Spirit Must Be in Fellowship with God's Spirit

- God's Holy Spirit is sent to indwell every believer. He indwells us in our spirit. It is there that communication must take place, but that is possible only as we are:
  - Aware of His presence
  - Yielded to His control
  - Pure in outward action and inward motive

- According to 1 Thessalonians 5:19, what can a Christian do that temporarily disqualifies him from worship? _____ _____Only one thing quenches His working in us—sin.

- Note that John 4 states that we must worship Him in "spirit and in truth." *Truth* refers to the Word of God. God's Spirit has always operated through the Word. Therefore, I am to take His Word through meditation—through my mind, will, and emotions—and then literally pray the Scriptures back to God. As I do so, I am worshipping God through the only channel in which true worship is possible.

- During this lesson, choose some of the promises of God and other passages that deal with the greatness and goodness of God, and "pray them back to Him." Truly worship Him the way He told the Samaritan woman He had to be worshipped.

Notes from the Teacher's Lesson

Nature of God:
- His essence— _____
  _____
- His attributes—_____
  _____

God is _____
- Stated: _____
- Described: _____
  _____
- Significance: _____
  _____
- Worship is _____
  _____

God is _____
- Attributes of personality: _____
  _____
- Significance: _____
  _____

Application Activities

1. Read and meditate on Psalm 104. Not only record all of the things you learn of God in this passage but also meditate on them and pray them back to the Father. Thank Him for what He is like, and apply to your life the things you learn about Him. Remember, you can write down all of these facts *about* God and yet never get to *know God*. It is only through meditation that knowledge *about* God is turned into knowledge *of* God.

2. Read about and meditate upon God and His dealings with Abraham in Genesis 12:10–20. Category: Bible Characters. Note: Worship God in spirit by praying back to Him the truths you learn from this project.

3. Our worship of God must be "in spirit and in truth." Discuss characteristics of the following means of worship that will ensure that they are acceptable to God (i.e., are performed in spirit and in truth):
   • Prayer
   • Singing (praise)
   • Bible study
   • Witnessing
   • Practical types of service (give examples of such services)

4. Study the account of the sacrifices of Cain and Abel in Genesis 4. Explain what it was about Abel's sacrifice that made it *acceptable* to God, and what it was about Cain's sacrifice that made it *unacceptable* to God? What applications to our own lives (especially to our worship) can we make of this account?

CHAPTER 9

GOD'S UNITY

"If there be but one God, then there is but One whom you need chiefly to study to please, and that is God."

—Thomas Watson, *A Body of Divinity*

Jeremy had a lot of friends as he grew through childhood and entered young manhood. Many of those friends were girls. After he came to realize that girls didn't really give boys cooties and that they could even at times help his team in the youth group win points, he was much more willing to befriend them.

By the time he had reached the upper grades of high school, he found himself viewing the young ladies in a much different way. They were not merely good point earners but also good friends. He developed close friendships with about three or four of them. By his graduation, however, he found himself increasingly attracted to one girl in particular. He wrote to Janice regularly when he went out of state to attend a Christian college, and he looked forward eagerly to being with her whenever he came home on vacation.

Although he was still friends with the other girls and occasionally dated them, Janice was a special friend. She was becoming so special, in fact, that he found himself wanting to date only her. This feeling increased when Janice enrolled a year later in the same Christian college. Jeremy still enjoyed the social contact and fellowship with other girls, but he had a different sense about Janice.

As he entered his senior year of college, Jeremy sensed a growing desire to be with Janice all the time. Wouldn't it be great if they could spend their entire lives together? He began praying earnestly about their relationship. He studied the Scriptures and found that the two of them agreed on every doctrine, and Janice seemed to fit all of the God–given qualifications for a godly help meet for him.

One day, after fortifying himself with courage, he "popped the question," asking Janice if she would marry him. Because she, too, had been experiencing the same feelings and had been praying about their relationship herself, Janice was not at all surprised by Jeremy's question; in fact, she had been expecting it and wondering why it was taking him so long to ask her. She feigned surprise, however, and replied excitedly, "Yes! Of course I'll marry you, Jeremy!"

Jeremy graduated at the end of that year. He got a job in town and worked hard, saving his money until Janice graduated the following year. Then they were married and began serving the Lord together and anticipating God's blessing of a future family.

A few weeks into married life, Jeremy found himself smiling to himself as he reflected on the changes that had occurred in his life over the last several months. He used to date a lot of female friends, and he sometimes had to do a lot of juggling to keep all of those different girls happy. He had to remember each of their interests, their schedules, their different tastes, and their different pet peeves to ensure that they had enjoyable dates. Now the only girl he had to please was Janice, and it was indeed a pleasure. He knew that he still had a lot to learn both about Janice herself (some of his married friends had jokingly warned him not to try to figure out women because it was an impossible task) and about being a godly husband for her. But he now had an entire lifetime to devote to one girl only—his wife.

His thoughts soon turned to how his new marriage was a clear spiritual metaphor. As a married man, he could love only one woman supremely; as a believer, he could worship and serve only one God. Just as it would be adultery to have affections for a woman other than Janice now, so it was spiritual adultery for him to set any other god before the one true God.

In both cases, absolute faithfulness was the expectation and demand. He could offer no less to his wife or his God.

Look up and read the following verses. Then fill in the blanks to complete them.

"Here, O Israel: the Lord our God is _____ Lord" (Deut. 6:4).

"Know therefore this day, and consider it in thine heart, that the Lord he is God in heaven above, and upon the earth beneath: there is _____ _____" (Deut. 4:39).

"Tell ye, and bring them near; yea, let them take counsel together: who hath declared this from ancient time? who hath told it from that time? have not I the Lord? and there is _____ _____; a just God and a Saviour, there is _____ _____" (Isa. 45:21).

The preceding verses teach the *only*–ness of God, that there is only one true God. The doctrine of God's *only*–ness is called the *unity* of God.

In the last lesson, you learned that God is _____ and _____. In this lesson, you continue your study of God's nature by discovering that God is *one*.

Notes from the Teacher's Lesson

Dr. Bob Jones, Sr., used to say, "If you will _____ _____ that you are going to settle every question on just _____ and that is the principle of _____, you have the victory already. Whenever you begin _____ _____ whether you are going to do the _____ thing or the _____ thing, you will end up doing the _____ thing."

- God is _____
- God's unity defined:_____

God's unity stated:

  In the Old Testament

  - _____
  - _____

  In the New Testament

  - _____
  - _____

The significance of God's unity:

Because there is one God, there is but One who deserves my undivided, wholehearted affection, and that is God (Deut. 6:4–5).

Student Work

The Proof of the Doctrine

Besides the fact that the Bible clearly states that there is one God, the following three obvious and logical facts point to one God.

There Can Be Only One "First Cause"

There must be a first cause that has its being of itself and on which all other beings depend. This first cause we call God. Obviously, there cannot be two *first* causes; only one can be first. So God gives life and motion to everything that exists.

How does Acts 17:28 point out this fact? _____
_____
_____

Since God is the First Cause, and there can be only one *first* cause, then there is only one God.

Only One Being Can Be Infinite

There cannot be two infinites. What does Jeremiah 23:24 ask? _____
_____
_____

If there be one infinite, which is filling all places at once, how can there be any room for another infinite to subsist? There can't!

There Can Be Only One Omnipotent Power

- If there were two omnipotents, then we would have a contest between these two: that which one would do, the other power, being equal, would oppose. How could *both* of them have *all* power? The very definition of God as having *all* power implies that there is only one God.

- What does Isaiah 44:6 say about this doctrine? _____
_____
_____
_____
_____

The Practice of the Doctrine

Of what significant use is this doctrine? We know there is one, and only one, God, but how is that fact important to you personally? Why do you need to know this truth?

If there is only one God, then the following points are true.

There Is Only One True Religion

Ephesians 4:5 states that there is "One Lord, one _____."
If there were many gods, then there might be many ways of salvation and many valid religions. Every god would be worshipped in his own way. But if there is but one God, there is but one way of salvation and one religion—one Lord, one faith.

Although we must respect individuals' political right to believe whichever religion they choose, we must not swallow Satan's lie, cloaked in the garb of "diversity," that all religions are equally valid. Some people say that we may be saved in any religion as long as we are sincere in our beliefs. But it would be absurd to imagine that God, who is One in essence, should appoint several religions in which He will be worshipped and several ways whereby we might be redeemed. There are many ways to hell, but there is only one road to heaven. That's why Christ said in John 14:6, "I am __

_____

_____ ."

Another verse that points to the fact of there being only one way of salvation is Acts 4:12, which says, "_____

_____

_____

_____ ."

Because there is only one true God, there is only one true religion—biblical Christianity. Although it might seem cruel and insensitive to preach and teach that all other religions are sending their adherents to hell, it is the truth, and we must be faithful witnesses to that truth.

There Is But One Whom We Need to Please

If there were many gods, then we should be hard put to please them all. What one god would like, the other gods would dislike. But there is only one God to please. Therefore, we must concentrate on pleasing Him.

What man had the testimony that he pleased God (see Heb. 11:5)?

_____

We please God in the following ways.

By Complying with His Will

- How did Christ express His desire to do the Father's will in John 4:34? _____

  _____

- Therefore, what did the Father say of Him in Matthew 3:17? __

  _____

  _____

- According to 1 Thessalonians 4:3, what is God's will for us? ____

  _____

- That is, that we should be holy. How do we become holy? _____

  _____

- How do we come to love Him? _____

  _____

- How do we get to know Him? _____

  _____

- When we are garnished with holiness, it is according to God's will, and He is pleased.

By Doing His Work

- What did Christ say in his high–priestly prayer (John 17:4) just before His crucifixion? _____

  _____

  _____

- Thomas Watson wrote, "Many people finish their lives, but do not finish their work." The work God has cut out for each person is much and varied, but all of our work falls into two categories:

  - Our duty toward God (to know, love, please, and glorify Him)
  - Our duty toward man (to get to know and love them, to win them to Christ, and to meet their needs)

    These two duties are found in Matthew 10:27. How are they stated in that verse? _____

    _____

    _____

    _____

By Dedicating Our Hearts to Give Him the Best of Everything

- How do we see this dedication in Abel's offering to God in Genesis 4:4? _____

  _____

- The sacrificial animals offered to God always had to be spotless and in perfect health. Why? Because there is but one great and mighty God; therefore, nothing less than our absolute *best* is fit for Him. If I give God halfhearted service, I dishonor Him. If I give God the leftovers of my time, talents, and money, I commit as gross a sin as one could commit.

- What perfect illustration of the homage and dedication we should give Him can be seen in the story of the baby Jesus? _____

_____

_____

There Is But One Whom We Must Love and Worship

Ephesians 4:6 states that this one God and Father is _____.
If our God is above all, then He must be loved and worshipped above all.
Our friends may have the milk of our love, but we must keep the cream for God. We must love Him as Asaph loved Him. How did Asaph express the quality of his love for God in Psalm 73:25? _____

_____

_____

Can you honestly say what Asaph said? Well did the songwriter pen the following words:

> Modern times have brought us many comforts;
> People live in wealth and luxury.
> But the Master still asks this question:
> "Lovest thou me, lovest thou me more than these?"

Our love is seen in our worship. Some people put everything before the Lord while claiming to love Him more than anything.

According to 2 Timothy 3:4, Some People Worship _____ More Than God

> This love could take the form of sports, recreations, thrills, socials, a weekend at the beach, a Sunday in the mountains, or a thousand other things. Does anything in your schedule interfere with your serving God *first*? Does anything keep you from your devotions, from memorizing Scripture, or from attending church *faithfully* on prayer meeting night and at all services on Sunday? If so, you have another god before the one true God!

According to 1 Timothy 6:9–10, Some People Worship _____ More Than God

According to Philippians 3:19, Some People Worship Their _____ More Than God

- The "belly" symbolizes sensual, lustful pleasures that some people are so determined to have that they sacrifice holiness and godliness to satisfy their fleshly appetites.

- What warning does God give in Psalm 16:4 to those who put another god before Him? _____
  _____
  _____
  _____
  _____

His Servants Should Be One

What was Christ's prayer in John 17:21? _____
_____

According to Acts 4:32, what was true of the first church? _____
_____
_____

Nothing makes a body of Christians more lovely, more exciting, or more admirable to the lost than to see them tied together with the heartstrings of love. Is there *anyone* to whom you are not now speaking, of whom you are jealous, or against whom you have *anything*? If so, you must go to him or her now. We all serve the same Lord, and we must serve Him together as one.

How saddened and sickened God must be to see youth groups divided according to the following groups:

- Couples
- Dating and nondating teens
- The schools they attend
- The way they dress or the brands of clothing they wear
- Whether they are athletes or cheerleaders
- The communities or the kinds of houses in which they live
- Who their best friends are

We Must Make God Our God

What does Psalm 48:14 say? _____

_____

What comfort can it be to hear that there is a God unless He is *our* God? Is He *your* God? Do you know Him through salvation? Do you know Him through meditation? Do you know Him through experience?

Read and memorize Psalm 63:1.

Application Activities

1. Read Psalm 106, and record all that you see about God in that chapter.

2. Record any providence (in either the personal, contemporary, or historical category) that sets forth the fact that there is a great God in heaven whom we must love and worship.

3. What implications does the doctrine of God's unity have for our prayer life? To whom are we to pray? What biblical conclusion can one make concerning the Roman Catholic practice of praying to Mary or to "the saints"?

4. Although the doctrine of God's unity implies that God's people are also to be united as one, why does it *not* condone the ecumenical movement, which encourages the unification of Protestants of all different shades with not only one another but also the Roman Catholic and Greek and Russian Orthodox churches, Muslims, Hindus, Buddhists, and other world religions?

CHAPTER 10

THE TRINITY

"It is limiting to God to confine Him within the narrow compass of our reason."

—Thomas Watson, *A Body of Divinity*

Craig was returning home from visiting his grandmother, and he had a lengthy layover at the airport before he began the last leg of his flight. As he sat in the lobby watching the airplanes land and take off, a member of a cult that seemed always to plague the airport approached him. Craig decided to try to witness to him.

At various points in their conversation, Craig mentioned Jesus Christ, God the Father, and the Holy Spirit. The cultist grabbed what he thought was his golden opportunity.

"So you believe that the Jesus Christ is God, right?" he asked.

"Yes, most definitely," Craig replied.

"And you also believe that the Father is God?"

"Yes, of course."

"And do you believe that the Holy Spirit is God, too?"

"Yes, they're all God."

"Well, then," the cultist concluded with a smile, "aren't you breaking the first of the Ten Commandments, 'Thou shalt have no other gods before me'? If all of these people are gods, then you have three gods!"

Craig sat stunned and silent. He could think of no response to prove his belief in the Trinity. He was relieved when at that moment he heard his flight called over the public address system.

How would you have responded to that cultist? Would you have been armed and able to defend your belief in the Trinity? This lesson is designed to show you how this doctrine is taught in both the Old and the New Testaments and the significance it plays in both salvation and living the Christian life.

Student Work

Having discussed the essence, personality, and unity of God, we can come to only one conclusion: there is no creature in the universe like our God. Truly He is unique among all beings. Nothing can compare with Him. This is one reason it is such a gross sin to liken God to or try to represent God by any type of image. Well did Ethan the Ezrahite ask in Psalm 89:6, "

_____

_____

_____

_____ ?"

Isaiah added (Isa. 55:8–9) that God is so exceedingly superior to all other created beings that His thoughts "_____

_____ neither are your _____ His _____,"
for His ways and thoughts are as different from our ways and thoughts as "_____."

In many ways, God is unique in all the universe, but in one aspect His uniqueness can hardly be explained adequately. That aspect is His Trinity. As David contemplated his God in Psalm 106:2, he asked, "Who can utter _____ "
and who can "_____ ?"

Therefore, we should approach the subject of the Trinity with a sense of awe and reverence. We should approach it as a diver approaches a "bottomless hole" in the ocean. We cannot explain or even fully understand it; we merely touch "the tip of the iceberg" or see the shallows of the unfathomable depths of God, and even that should be a thrill that we never forget.

The Doctrine of the Trinity

The doctrine of the Trinity has been believed from the first centuries of Christianity. It is one of the cardinal doctrines of the Bible and generally distinguishes fundamental theology from cults and liberalism.

Although the word *trinity* does not occur in the Bible, the truth is found throughout the Word. *Trinity* was coined by an early Latin Christian writer to identify the doctrine that "there is one only and true God, but in the unity of the godhead there are three eternal and co–equal persons, the same in substance but distinct in subsistence." (Note: *subsistence* means "being" or "existence.")

The Trinity is a divine riddle, where one makes three and three make one.

The Problem of the Trinity

Many people have opposed the doctrine of the Trinity through the centuries. Today, many cults claim that the doctrine is of the devil in that it teaches that there are three gods. Their argument reasons thus: "Is God the *Father* God? (yes) Is God the *Son* God? (yes) Is God the *Holy Spirit* God. (yes) Then you have three gods!"

Another argument against the Trinity is based on the fact that the word *trinity* does not occur in the Scriptures.

A third argument asks the believer to illustrate the Trinity. Of course, there is no *perfect* illustration. We can offer close facsimiles, but none of them is *exactly* like the mystery of three being one and yet one being three. And it is at this point that we see the beauty of the Trinity. God is unique. If someone tries to entrap you by getting you to illustrate the Trinity, don't fall into their snare. Rather, reply, "If there was something else in the universe to compare with this mystery, then God wouldn't be God." And then quote them Isaiah 40:18. Write this verse below, and then memorize it.

_____

_____

_____

_____

The Proof of the Trinity

The word *trinity* is perhaps not the best word to describe this doctrine because *trinity* defines only half of the doctrine. It has two parts: the unity of God (the oneness of God, which we studied earlier) and the threeness of God. Perhaps "tri–unity" would better state the full doctrine of the Trinity.

Old Testament Proof of the Trinity

The Old Testament emphasizes the "unity" aspect of the Trinity. State how this aspect is seen in each of the following verses.

- Exodus 20:3—_____
  _____
  _____

- Deuteronomy 6:4—_____
  _____
  _____

- Deuteronomy 4:35—_____
  _____
  _____

- Isaiah 45:14— _____
  _____
  _____

- Isaiah 46:9— _____
_____

However, the Old Testament clearly intimates in two ways that a plurality exists in this one God.

By the Use of the Word *Elohim*

- *Elohim* is the plural form of the Hebrew word *El*, meaning "God." Note its unusual occurrence in the following verse.

- Deuteronomy 6:4—"The Lord (*Jehovah*) our God (*Elohim*) is one Lord (*Jehovah*)."

- What is unique about this statement? _____
_____

- This verse is not the only place where *Elohim* is used. In fact, it is God's most common Old Testament name!

By the Use of the Plural Pronouns *Us* and *Our*

- Genesis 1:26 – "Let *us* make man in *our* image, after *our* likeness."

- Genesis 11:7 – "Let *us* go down."

- Isaiah 6:8 – "Whom shall I send, and who will go for *us*?"

Look up these three passages and be able to identify both the reference and the event taking place in each instance.

New Testament Proof of the Trinity

The New Testament concentrates not so much on the unity of God as on the three in one. Thus, the three persons are seen in each of the following six events. Complete the following table by stating how each person is involved in these events.

New Testament Events That Illustrate the Trinity			
Event & Reference	Father	Son	Holy Spirit
The incarnation of Christ (Luke 1:35)			
The baptism of Christ (Matt. 3:16–17)			
The atonement (Heb. 9:14)			
The resurrection of Christ (Acts 2:32; John 10:17–18; Rom. 1:4)			
The salvation of the soul (1 Pet. 1:2)			
The Great Commission (Matt. 28:19; Note: name is singular)			

Application of the Doctrine

Four major uses are made of the doctrine of the Trinity.

It Separates Those Who Live by Faith from Those Who Live by Reason

The doctrine of the Trinity separates those who live by reason and intellect from those who live by faith. The Trinity is purely a doctrine of faith; the plumb line of reason is too short to fathom this mystery, but, as Thomas Watson wrote, "Where reason cannot wade, there faith may swim." Some Bible truths may be demonstrated by reason, such as the fact that there is a God. But the Trinity of persons in the unity of essence is wholly supernatural and must be believed by faith. Watson declared that this great doctrine "is not against reason, but above it." The great philosophers, doctors, and scientists who could discover the stars and place man on the moon could never, by their deepest search, find the mystery of the Trinity. It is this doctrine that separates those who truly live by faith from those who operate solely by reason. Those who are most offended by the doctrine of the Trinity are not operating on the principle of faith.

It Calls for Equal Reverence

There is not more or less of God in any person of the Godhead. The Father is not more God than the Son or the Holy Spirit. No one person in the Trinity has a supereminence above another.

What does John 5:23 say in reference to this issue? _____

_____

_____

It Calls for Equal Obedience

Because all three persons of the Trinity are equal, we must obey one as readily as the other two persons of the Trinity.

It Illustrates God's Total Difference from Man

At the beginning of this lesson, we noted Isaiah 55:8–9. Now let's apply it to our lives. The following chart shows how man operates (left–hand column). The verse in the right–hand column shows, by contrast, how God operates in the same situation. (Complete the chart as part of the "Application Activities.")

God's Way Is Not Man's Way	
Man's way	God's way
1. The way to greatness is to become a leader.	Matthew 23:11 (Be a _____ .)
2. The way to gain independence and honor is to get out from under authority.	Proverbs 15:33 (Before honor is _____ .)
3. The way to gain acceptance is to cover your mistakes.	Proverbs 28:13 (Confess and _____ them.)
4. One who dedicates his life to God loses it.	Matthew 16:25 (One who saves his life will _____ it; one who loses his life for God's sake will _____ it.)
5. We get even with our enemies either by doing to them what they did to us or by avoiding them.	Matthew 5:44 (Love, do good to, and pray for _____ .)
6. Man is basically good.	Romans 3:10, 23 (There is none _____ , all have sinned.)
7. The "good Lord" overlooks our faults.	Romans 6:23 (The wages of sin is _____ .)
8. If we sincerely try to do right, God will surely take us to heaven.	Ephesians 2:8–9 (We're saved by _____ , a gift of God, not by works.)
9. The pain we go through on earth is God's only "hell."	Luke 16:22–23 (Note which came first.) (In hell the rich man lifted up his _____ , being in torment.)
10. I've "always" been a Christian.	John 3:36 (He who believes on the Son has _____ ; he who doesn't believe shall not see life but has the wrath of God.)

Notes from the Teacher's Lesson

God is _____

The Trinity defined: there are three eternal distinctions in one divine essence, known respectively as the Father, the Son, and the Holy Spirit.

The Trinity stated:

1. In the Old Testament

    _____

2. In the New Testament

    • _____

    • _____

    • _____

The Significance of the Trinity: _____

_____

_____

_____

In Salvation:_____

    • _____

    • _____

    • _____

In Christian Living:

    • _____

    _____

    _____

    • _____

    • _____

Application Activities

1. On the preceding chart (contrasting man's way with God's way), record (from the references in the right hand column) what God's way

is in contrast to man's way. Using this outline of God's way, learn to operate as God operates.

2. Conduct a study of the personal providences you've seen in your life during the past five years. Write a brief explanation of each providence.

3. Conduct a study of the following groups that deny the Trinity and explain the specific aspects of the Trinity that they reject. Then explain why their arguments are erroneous. (Use Scripture as well as logic to support your explanation.)
   - Jews
   - Moslems
   - Socinians
   - Arians

4. Explain how the Holy Spirit performs holiness in believers. (Use appropriate Scripture support for your explanation.)

UNIT 3
THE ATTRIBUTES OF GOD

"God's glory lies chiefly in His attributes, which are the several beams by which the divine nature shines forth."

—Thomas Watson, *A Body of Divinity*

CHAPTER 11

HIS OMNISCIENCE

"If God be infinitely wise, let us go to Him for wisdom, as Solomon did."

—Thomas Watson, *A Body of Divinity*

Ron was young, healthy, had a lovely wife and family, and was serving the Lord faithfully. Yet, his doctor was telling him that he had a cancerous tumor in his eye. Surgery was essential to save his life, but that surgery would cost him his eye.

How could this be happening? Did God know what He was doing? This tragedy could end—or at least seriously hinder—his small ministry for the Lord through music.

In spite of facing this severe test of his faith, Ron knew that God knows all things and always does what is for both the good of His children and His own glory. Although he couldn't understand God's reasons for what He was doing to him, Ron rested quietly and confidently in the Lord. He let the doctors remove his eye. He would take life one day at a time and leave the future in God's hands.

During his recovery from the surgery, Ron took comfort in meditating on the words of Job 23:10: "But he knoweth the way that I take: when he hath tried me, I shall come forth as gold." Later, he set those sentiments to music: "O rejoice in the Lord, He makes no mistake. He knoweth the end of each path that I take."

The rest is history. Ron altered his music ministry a little, becoming "Patch the Pirate." Through the loss of his eye, God began to use Ron Hamilton to reach multiplied thousands of people, young and old alike, for Himself, leading some to salvation and encouraging others to trust in the Lord to get them through their own unique trials. His radio program *The Adventures of Patch the Pirate* is heard weekly on more than 230 stations in the United States and several foreign countries. More than 15,000 children participate in Patch the Pirate clubs.

God knew *exactly* what He was doing with Ron's life by taking his eye— and He knows what He's doing with *your* life, too. In fact, God knows *all things*! That attribute—God's all-knowingness, or omniscience—is the topic of this lesson.

Having discussed the nature of God in the three preceding lessons, we come now to the attributes of God. An attribute is simply *a characteristic of God that describes what God is like*. The several lessons in this unit deal with each of God's various attributes.

We may divide God's attributes into two categories: natural attributes and moral attributes. From the teacher's lesson, you will learn the following things about God's attributes.

Notes from the Teacher's Lesson

The Attributes of God Categorized and Listed	
Natural Attributes	Moral Attributes
1. Omniscience	1.
2. Omnipresence	2.
3. Omnipotence	3.
4. Immutability	4.
5. Eternality	

In this lesson we are studying God's omniscience.

- The definition of *omniscience*: _____
  _____

- The statement of omniscience: _____

- The significance of omniscience:

  - To sinners— _____
    _____
    _____

  - To saints— _____
    _____
    _____

Student Work

Stated negatively, God's omniscience means that God knows—and has always known—everything. He has never learned and cannot learn! God is so far superior to man that it is sometimes easier to understand Him by discussing what He is *not* like. Scripture sometimes uses such a negative approach to help us understand a God who is far superior to human reason.

Note, for example, Isaiah 40:13–14. How is God's omniscience seen in those verses? _____
_____
_____

If God ever had to learn from someone else, then He would not be God.

We might also state that God's omniscience means that He knows no one thing better than any other. He never discovers anything. He is never surprised. He never wonders.

Omniscience Illustrated

The Bible abounds with stories and incidents in which we see God's omniscience. Note the following examples.

In Creation

According to Psalm 104:24, how did God make the earth? _____
_____

Thomas Watson said, "None but a wise God could so curiously contrive the world." We may see the "wisdom of God blazing in the sun, twinkling in the stars… in marshalling and ordering everything in its proper place and sphere. If the sun had been set lower, it would have burnt us; if higher, it would not have warmed us with its beams. God's wisdom is seen in appointing the seasons of the year."

What does Psalm 74:17 say about this fact? _____
_____

"If it had been all summer," Watson explained, "the heat would have scorched us; if all winter, the cold would have killed us. If it had been all night, there had been no labour; if all day, there had been no rest. The wisdom of God is seen in preparing and ripening the fruits of the earth, in the wind and frost that prepare the fruits, and in the sun and rain that ripen the fruits."

In Redemption

Here is God's masterpiece of omniscience, "to contrive a way to happiness between the sin of man and the justice of God" (Watson). Mercy and grace had a mind to save sinners, but God's justice was just as determined that man's sin be punished. If God forgave the sinner, God's justice was offended. If He condemned the sinner to hell, His love, mercy, and grace were wronged. What could be done to save the sinner and yet satisfy justice?

Only the wisdom of God should offer such an answer. While mercy and justice were debating how it should be done, the wisdom of God stepped in and thus spake: "Let God become man; let the Son of God come to earth robed in human flesh and suffer for man's sin." Watson says, "What wisdom was this, that Christ should be made sin, yet know no sin; that God should condemn sin, yet save the sinner! Here is wisdom, *to find out the way of salvation*."

In His Providences

"Every providence," Watson declared, "has a mercy or a wonder wrapped up in it." We see the wisdom of God in His works of providence in the following ways.

By Accomplishing Great Things by Small Means

He cured the snake–bitten Israelites with a look at a bronze snake on a pole. He used a small stone to destroy Goliath. He used the breaking of pitchers to destroy completely the Midianites of Gideon's day. As Watson said, "The less probability in the instrument, the more is God's wisdom seen."

By Doing What Seems Opposite to Man's Doings

- One illustration of this truth is the advancement of Joseph. God advanced Joseph (see Gen. 39:20) by having him:
  - Thrown into a pit
  - Sold to the Ishmaelites
  - Accused falsely of adultery
  - Thrown into prison as a result of those accusations
- His imprisonment made the way for his advancement. Eventually, Joseph was next in command to Pharaoh and, thus, in God's glorious wisdom, Israel was protected and preserved during famine in Egypt. As a result, they grew into a great nation.

- A second illustration of this truth is Gideon's army. When God wanted Israel to be victorious over the Midianites, what way did He take to accomplish that end? He *decreased* the size of Gideon's army! Again, He worked opposite of the way we would work. We would have *increased* his army. "The people that are with thee are too many" (Judg. 7:2). God reduced the original army of 32,000 to an army of 300. By taking away the apparent means of victory, He made Israel depend on Him and thus gain the victory.

By Making Evil Turn to Good

- Just as several poisonous ingredients, when mixed by a skilled druggist, turn into a helpful medicine, so God takes the most deadly actions of evil men and uses them for the good of His children. In 2 Corinthians 4:17, what did Paul's affliction do?

  _____

  _____

- According to Genesis 50:20, Joseph's brothers meant him _____ when they sold him to the Ishmaelites, but God _____ _____ and thereby used it to _____ _____ (Gen. 50:20).

In His Prophetic Utterances

God's omniscience is perhaps seen most clearly in His prophecy concerning future events. How do we see God's omniscience in the following passages?
- Genesis 15:13— _____

  _____

- Isaiah 7:14; Micah 5:2— _____

  _____

  _____

- Jeremiah 29:10; 2 Chronicles 36:14–21—_____

  _____

  _____

Omniscience Applied

To what use can we put this great doctrine? We can find many uses for it, but in this lesson we will consider only the following applications.

It Delights the Saint

The omniscience of God should bring joy and delight to believers for at least three reasons.

He Knows the Worst About Us but Still Saved Us

- Psalm 103:14 says that He "knows our _____"
  and "remembers _____ ."
  In human relationships, we often fear that something about us
  might come to light to break the relationship, so we always try
  to put on our best face with others. But God already knows the
  worst about us. And still He saved us! This is further proof of the
  doctrine of "eternal security" (once saved, always saved).

- How does the fact that God knows *all* things (past, present, and
  future) and that He knows the *worst* things about us but still saved us
  prove the fact that we are saved forever and can never be lost? __
  _____
  _____

He Knows the Best About Us When Others Aren't Even Aware

- At times, our best activity for God goes unnoticed by those
  around us. They offer us no thanks or appreciation. No one seems
  to care. At other times, our actions are misjudged, and we are
  severely criticized for something we did not intend. At yet other
  times, when things that we've not anticipated go wrong, we are
  looked upon as failures. Then people—even our friends—say,
  "How could so–and–so do a thing like that? I would have thought
  better of him." They don't know our situation or our heart. They
  are critical, and nothing we can do or say seems to change their
  opinion. What then?

- There is comfort in knowing that God, who knows all things, also knows us. God knows our weaknesses and sin, our frailties and humanness. But He also knows when we are trying. He knows when we are putting forth our best efforts for Him.

He Knows What He Is Going to Make of Us

God has a purpose in mind for each of us, and He saved us for that purpose. We have seen something of that purpose in our Master Chart from Lesson 2. He brings glory to Himself by making us holy. Romans 8:28–29 defines this as being "conformed to the image of His Son." To this end God is determined to bring us. Although we fall and fail, sin and slip, God is still working—even through our failures—to make us like His Son. Thus, we should ever look to Him who in His wisdom will one day present us before His throne as blameless, spotless, and pure.

It Comforts Us in Difficulties

How did God's omniscience comfort Job in his trials (Job 23:10)?

_____

_____

_____

God knows every trial, tribulation, sorrow, and heartache and allows them in His glorious wisdom. He is using them for our good.

It Causes Us to Let Him Make Our Decisions for Us

God knows all of the pitfalls as well as the ways for us to be happy in life. He not only knows every path and every combination of paths that can be taken and where they all lead but also has offered to guide us through the maze of life! To refuse His direction and try to make it on our own is sheer folly! Yet, how often do we make decisions without once consulting Him?

It Guards Us Against Sin

Nothing is more sobering to the human mind than the thought that God is watching us. This thought should be uppermost in our minds when we are beset with temptation. David said that he could not escape the eye of God even in the darkness (Ps. 139:11–12).

When Sarah drove Hagar into the wilderness, the Lord appeared to Hagar and spoke to her. She was so overwhelmed at this unexpected appearance by God that she exclaimed, "La Hai Roi"—"Thou, God, seest me." In Genesis 16:14, she named the well that marked the spot *Beer–lahai–roi* as a continual reminder that God sees and knows all.

May we be sobered by the thought that every sin is known to God. Every evil thought is as loud in His ears as if we had shouted it from the house-top. Every wrong motive is as plain to Him as the back of our own hand is to us. He *knows* us!

Application Activities

1. Read Psalm 139 and record all of the things you learn about God's omniscience in those verses. Note especially verses 1–6 and 14–24.

2. Complete a personal providence description concerning any event in your life that, at the time it happened, you could not understand at all what good could come of it, yet looking back on it now you see how God knew what He was doing.

3. Conduct a detailed study of the life of Ron Hamilton ("Patch the Pirate") to learn more about how he learned to trust in the omniscience of God during his affliction. Trace the growth and development of his music ministry after the loss of his eye. Talk to people who have been blessed by his ministries to determine how they, too, learned to trust more in God as a result of Ron's testimony.

4. Find other instances (perhaps in your own family, church, or school) of people who learned from personal tragedies or setbacks that God, in His omniscience, knows all things and used even those trials to conform them to the image of Christ and glorify Himself.

5. Read *Comeback*, *When You Can't Come Back*, and/or *The Worth of a Man* by former San Francisco Giants pitcher Dave Dravecky.

Summarize—either orally or in writing—some of the spiritual lessons that he learned from his career–ending cancer. (Bibliographic data for each of these books are given in the Recommended Reading List. These books are listed in the order in which Dravecky wrote them; therefore, they should be read in that order to get the most from them.)

6. Read *Rise and Walk* by former New York Jets defensive end Dennis Byrd. Summarize—either orally or in writing—some of the spiritual lessons that he learned from his career–ending injury in a pro football game. (Bibliographic data are given in the Recommended Reading List.)

CHAPTER 12

HIS OMNIPRESENCE

"God's essence is not limited either to the regions above, or to the terrestrial globe, but is everywhere."

—Thomas Watson, *A Body of Divinity*

Joy was home alone. Her parents, sister, and two brothers were away for the afternoon, and the house was very quiet. Joy decided that it was a perfect time to catch up on some of her letter writing.

She finished hand writing one letter to a missionary friend and was just beginning a letter to one of her numerous foreign pen pals when she suddenly sensed a strangeness in the room. The quiet house had become even quieter, and the silence was eerie. Something was missing.

Gradually, Joy realized what the missing "something" was. The clock radio on the end table across the room was not humming. The fan of the computer in front of her on the desk was not turning. The refrigerator a few feet away in the kitchen was not running. The electricity had gone off.

She had become so used to having the consistent hum and whir of electrical appliances around her that she never really noticed it any more—until the power went out, then the silence was very obvious. She chuckled to herself momentarily, but then she got serious again.

How like our unawareness of God's presence, she thought. *We know He's always with us—in fact, we know He's everywhere—but we get so caught up with everything else in life that we fail to sense His presence with us. I'm sure glad that* He *doesn't leave us like the when the power occasionally goes out!*

In Genesis 28, we read the account of Jacob's dream, in which God told him, "I am with thee, and will keep thee in all places whither thou goest, and will bring thee again into this land; for I will not leave thee, until I have done that which I have spoken to thee of" (v. 15). In the next verse, Jacob awoke. Remembering vividly the dream he had just had, his first reaction was to exclaim, "Surely the Lord is in this place; and I knew it not."

The Bible teaches that God is *everywhere* and *in everything*. That doctrine is called God's *omnipresence*. A full realization of the truth of this doctrine can have a greater impact on your life than if all of the power went out on the darkest, coldest night of the year. Yet, Hannah Whitall Smith wrote, "One of the greatest obstacles to an unwavering experience in the interior life is the difficulty of seeing God in everything."

During this lesson, ask God to increase your awareness of His presence, then *practice* the presence of God daily.

Notes from the Teacher's Lesson

The definition of *omnipresence*: _____
_____

The statement of omnipresence:_____
_____

Does God occupy uninhabited places? _____
_____
_____

What's the difference between omnipresence and pantheism?
- Pantheism— _____
- Omnipresence— _____

The Significance of Omnipresence

No One Can _____ **God**

- Running: _____
  _____

- Hiding: _____
  _____

God _____ **All and** _____ **All**

The heart and attitude of kings and all in authority—_____
_____
_____

The heart of every person:

- 1 Samuel 16:7— _____
  _____

- 1 Kings 4:29— _____
  _____

- Job 23:16— _____
  _____

- Psalm 7:9— _____
  _____

- Proverbs 21:1— _____
  _____

- Isaiah 57:15— _____
  _____

- Jeremiah 24:7— _____
  _____

- Malachi 4:6— _____
  _____

- Hebrews 4:12—_____

  _____

- Ephesians 3:17—_____

  _____

**God Is Present in Every Christian, So We Should_____
Living in His _____**

Student Work

Truths Learned from Scripture

The following passages are among the chief verses revealing the main truths concerning God's omnipresence. Read and study each verse or passage carefully. Then place the correct reference beside the appropriate statement (some references will be used more than once).

1.		Men under God's wrath seek to hide from His presence.	A. Psalm 139:7–12
2.		Even good men try to run from God.	B. Jeremiah 23:23–24
			C. Matthew 28:20
3.		God sees as well in darkness as in light.	D. Amos 9:2–4
4.		Those who worship other gods don't know where their gods are or what they are doing.	E. Isaiah 66:1
			F. 1 Kings 8:27
5.		God fills all of heaven and earth.	G. 1 Kings 18:27
6.		God is so immense that He can sit in heaven and place His feet on the earth.	H. Jeremiah 5:22
			I. Jonah 1:3
7.		There are no secret places to hide where God's eyes will not see.	J. 1 Corinthians 6:19
8.		God's physical presence keeps the sea in its place.	K. Revelation 6:16
9.		God is in every Christian.	
10.		God is in heaven and hell.	
11.		God's presence should cause us to fear the Lord.	
12.		God is at the bottom of the sea.	
13.		When a man seeks to flee from God's presence, he starts down and ends up paying a terrible fare (price).	
14.		The ocean boundaries are a testimony of the very presence of God all along the coastline.	
15.		No building can be called the sole house of God, for the whole universe is God's house.	
16.		God is always with His children, especially when we are serving Him.	

Practical Uses of This Truth

A consciousness of His presence will bring...

- Comfort and fellowship in loneliness (Matt. 28:19–20)

- Faith in impossible situations or when you are totally misun-derstood (1 Sam. 30:6), (How does this verse reveal this truth?)

  _____

  _____

  _____

  _____

- Protection in danger (Ps. 91:9–16)

- Victory over temptation.

Again, the words *la–hai–roi* are important. God sees and knows all and will judge all.

Application Activities

1. Read Psalm 139 and record all of the things you learn about God's omnipresence. In how many different places did the author note God's presence? What important lessons did he learn (and can we derive) from this psalm? (Note especially verses 3, 5, 7–13, and 15–16.)

2. Meditate on the providence of God in the life of a contemporary in which the *presence* of God was a key factor. Write a summary of the incident and share it with the class.

3. Read chapter 12 of Hannah Whitall Smith's classic work *The Christian's Secret of a Happy Life* ("Is God in Everything?"). (Bibliographic data are given in the Recommended Reading List.) Report on the impor-tant lessons offered by this short selection.

CHAPTER 13

HIS OMNIPOTENCE

"[God] can do what he will; his power is as large as his will."

—Thomas Watson, *A Body of Divinity*

Raymond sat upright in bed with a sudden start. His heart was racing wildly, and he found himself gasping for air.

His sudden reaction had been prompted by a horrific clap of thunder and a blinding flash of lightning. A severe thunderstorm had suddenly arisen shortly after he had fallen asleep. He had slept calmly as the storm approached his neighborhood; he never heard the gradually increasing rumble of the thunder. But then a bolt of lightning had struck a large tree in his neighbor's yard, and he was suddenly and unceremoniously awakened from his dreams.

He hopped out of bed and flew to the bedroom window just as a gust of wind blew a heavy mist of rainwater into the room. He hurriedly closed the window and wiped the water from the sill. Then he stood gazing out at the raging storm.

Raymond loved to watch thunderstorms. As he stood before the window, he marveled at the vivid blasts of light that illuminated everything in the neighborhood as though it were midday. Then everything was swallowed up with an inky darkness that seemed even darker because of the brightness of the lightning. The crashing thunder that accompanied each lightning flash shook the entire house.

"Ray!" His father burst into his room. "Get downstairs—NOW!"

"Why? What's the matter, Pop?" Raymond asked. "Isn't this storm cool? The lightning is just aweso...."

"NOW, Ray! We don't have time to watch. A tornado is coming! Get downstairs fast!"

His father ran down the hallway, yelling to alert the other children and grabbing every flashlight he could find. They all obediently streamed down the stairs and into the basement. Just as they closed the basement door behind them, they all heard a terrible roar, much louder and more sustained than even the loudest thunderbolt they had heard before. There were loud bangs and creaks from upstairs, followed by sudden breaking of glass and more roaring. They could feel the drop in air pressure even in the basement. Then it was suddenly quiet.

Raymond's father flipped on the radio. After a few minutes, the announcer declared that the tornado had left their community. It was once again safe to go upstairs.

The power was out, but in the glare of their flashlights they could see that the picture window in the living room had been shattered. Rain had blown in, soaking the carpet. The drapes hung in tatters, part inside and part outside the house.

Raymond walked over to the window and looked out toward the neighbor's house across the street. Sparks were arcing from a nearby transformer. In the intermittent flashes of lightning he saw a debris–covered lot where the neighbor's two–story house had stood just moments earlier.

Later, when daylight finally arrived, they went outside to survey the damage to the community. Their house sustained only minor damage in contrast to several houses on the opposite side of the street. The roofs of many houses had been ripped away. Some of the two–stories were now minus the upper levels. And a few houses, like the one across the street, were simply blown away; only foundation blocks remained to show rescue workers and news crews where homes had once stood.

"Wow!" Raymond exclaimed. "This is something else! Look at how it wiped out that house, just barely touched ours, and then didn't even raise a shingle on those two over there!"

"This," his father said quietly, "is just a taste of the power of God. Remember the awe you feel at this moment."

This lesson deals with the third of God's natural attributes—His omnipotence, or His awesome power.

Notes from the Teacher's Lesson

God is omnipotent.

The definition of *omnipotence*:

- Negatively— _____
  _____

- Positively— _____
  _____

The statement of omnipotence: _____

The significance of omnipotence:_____

_____

- _____
- _____
- _____

Student Work

Scripture References for Omnipotence

Look up and read the following references, then match each reference with the appropriate statement about God's omnipotence (some references will be used more than once).

1.		The heavenly hosts praise God for His omnipotence and state that He will reign over all creatures.	A. Revelation 19:6
2.		Another way of saying that God is omnipotent is to say that He is almighty. Almighty is the name God uses for Himself.	B. Isaiah 46:10–11 C. Daniel 4:35
3.		Almighty comes from the Hebrew word El Shaddai, which occurs some fifty–six times in the Bible. To say that God is omnipotent is to say that God can do everything.	D. Psalm 33:6–9 E. Colossians 1:17
4.		Therefore, nothing is too hard for Him.	F. Job 42:2
5.		There are some things that God will not do. For example, He will not—indeed cannot—lie). However, God can do anything He wills.	G. Ephesians 3:20–21 H. Genesis 17:1
6.		Furthermore, God not only can do what He wills but also will do all that He has determined to do (by His counsels), and no one can stop His hand.	I. Jeremiah 32:17 J. Isaiah 40:28
7.		God's power is seen in that He made all things by His spoken Word.	
8.		In fact, gravity is nothing but the unseen power holding all things together.	
9.		God's power is so great that it is inexhaustible. That is, He never gets tired.	
10.		Compared with God, we poor creatures are nothing.	
11.		Who are we ever to question Him? No one has a right to ever question His rights.	
12.		In fact, there is no need to question Him for He can and will do far more for us than we could ever imagine.	
13.		Therefore, a realization of God's omnipotence should produce awe and respect for our all–powerful God.	

Manifestations of Omnipotence

God's omnipotence is seen in the following six major areas.

Over Creation and Nature

Over Creation

- He needs no instrument with which to work; He can work without tools.
- He needs no matter with which to work; He creates matter and then works on it.
- He need expend no labor to work; He "spake, and _____ " (Ps. 33:9).

Over Nature

State how God's power is seen over the following elements.

- Mountains and hills (Nah. 1:5–6) _____

_____

_____

- Wind and water (Ps. 107:23–29) _____

_____

_____

- Fire (Dan. 3:19–25) _____

_____

_____

- Sun (Isa. 38:8) _____

_____

- Animals (Dan. 6:22) _____

_____

Over Angels

How do we see this fact in Hebrews 1:14? _____
_____
_____

Over Men

How do we see this fact in Daniel 4:35? _____
_____
_____
_____
_____

Over Satan

How is God's power over Satan suggested in the following verses?

- Job 1:12; 2:6 _____
_____
_____

- Luke 22:31–32 _____
_____

  Note: Peter was saved from Satan by God's power, and he didn't even know there was a battle being fought! We would probably quake if we could see the battles being waged for our souls in the spiritual realm! Thank God He is all–powerful.

- Revelation 20:2 _____
_____

Over History

Daniel's dreams in Daniel 7–9 reveal in a striking way God's complete mastery over the history of the world. We need never wonder or worry when we see dark clouds mount or hear war cries. Our God is in control and is bringing every event to the fulfillment of the time when He will come again for the saints and will finally sit as the omnipotent Ruler of all nations.

Over Redemption

The same power that drew Christ from the grave draws sinners from sin to salvation. Someone has said, "Greater power is put forth in conversion than in creation. In conversion [God] faces opposition, while in creation He faced no opposition." In creation He works but one miracle, but in conversion He works many miracles, including the following:

- The blind are made to see
- The dead are raised to life in Christ
- The deaf hear the voice of the Son of God

Creation was the work of God's _____
(a part of His body, Ps. 8:3), but conversion is the work of God's
_____ (a different part of His body, Luke 1:51).
O, the infinite power of Jehovah! To save a poor sinner and to transform him into a very child of this holy and immaculate God is beyond comprehension!

Practical Uses of His Omnipotence

Of what use is this great truth to us? Read the following verses and state in your own words what the knowledge of His omnipotence as shown in each reference should mean to you.

- 1 Peter 1:5 _____
  _____
  _____

- Psalm 33:6–8 _____
  _____
  _____

- 2 Corinthians 9:8 and 1 Thessalonians 5:24 _____
  _____
  _____
  _____

In particular, God will give you power to (1) overcome those sins that now bind you, (2) overcome any temptation, and (3) do anything He asks of you.

- Genesis 50:20; Job 1:12; 2:6 _____
  _____
  _____
  _____

- Romans 12:1–2 – Our most reasonable act is to _____
  _____
  _____
  _____
  _____
  _____ .

Teens need never doubt or fear. God is in control. But better than that is the fact that the God who is in control is a *good* God and is working everything for our joy and benefit! He isn't trying to hurt us or make us walk a severe, dull life. Many people think that if they yield to God's plan they will be miserable all their lives. If they only knew that all of God's power is in reserve to *bless* us and make us exceedingly happy and joyous. Paul said, "The _____ of _____ leadeth thee to _____" (Rom. 2:4).

Application Activities

1. Read Psalm 33 and list all of the things you see about your wonderful God in this passage. *Pray* the passage back to God, and in meditation thank Him for who He is.

2. Meditate on a providence of God concerning His omnipotence as seen in any story in the book of Daniel (Category: Bible Character or History).

3. Conduct a study of the name *El Shaddai*, one of the names of God. Give at least one Scripture example *and* one personal example from

your own (or your immediate family's) life in which the power of God has been used in the following ways:

- To protect
- To provide
- To fulfill a promise
- To encourage

4. Read Psalm 107:23–43. Note particularly the psalmist's comments about how sailors see and experience God's power on the seas. List other awe–inspiring events or wonders of nature that have prompted you to declare the awesome omnipotence of God. Explain why unbelievers can witness the same things and yet *not* give glory to God for them.

CHAPTER 14

HIS ETERNALITY

"Study God's eternity, it will make us adore where we cannot fathom."
—Thomas Watson, *A Body of Divinity*

Light travels at the phenomenal speed of 186,000 miles per second. Scientists refer to the distance that light can travel at that speed in one year—approximately 6,000,000,000,000 (that's six *trillion*) miles—as *one* light-year. The closest star to our sun, Alpha Centauri, is 4.326 light-years from us. That means that if we could travel at the speed of light (a pretty big *if*, wouldn't you agree?), it would take us about four years and a few months to get to it!

The star Arcturus is about thirty-seven light-years from us. Spica is more than 200 light-years away. Deneb, the brightest star of the constellation Cygnus, is about 1,500 light-years away. And all of those stars are just a tiny part of the objects in outer space that make up the galaxy of which our solar system is a part—the Milky Way.

The Milky Way is estimated to be 15,000 light-years thick and 100,000 light-years in diameter. Within this vast galaxy, our solar system is located about 30,000 light-years from the center. And beyond our galaxy are other galaxies. At least twenty different galaxies are nearest to us in what astronomers call the "Local Group." In that group is the Andromeda Galaxy, which is about 2,200,000 light-years away.

"Wow! Astronomical!" you might be saying (if you're still with me). Well, hold onto your hat; there's more!

Evidence has been found of galaxies at 350 million light–years from us, and even they are not the end of outer space! Astronomers say that beyond the most distant galaxies are quasi–stellar objects (called *quasars* for short). Most astronomers believe that these objects are about *five billion* light–years from us! They seem to be traveling away from us (our "expanding universe") at about 80 percent of the speed of light. (If they were traveling *at* the speed of light, we would never be able to tell it because they would be traveling too fast for their light to reach us!)

Is your mind boggled now? It's hard for us to comprehend times and distances of such magnitude. Some of us are hard pressed to comprehend what happened in 586 BC—or even in the class discussion last week. Comprehending the concept of light–years is far beyond what we can think or imagine. We must say with David, "When I consider thy heavens, the work of thy fingers, the moon and the stars, which thou hast ordained; What is man, that thou art mindful of him? (Ps. 8:3–4*a*).

Now try to imagine eternity. No beginning. No end. No time at all.

That's God. He is eternal. This lesson is concerned with focusing our attention on this mind–boggling attribute of God.

Notes from the Teacher's Lesson

The definition of *eternality*: _____
_____
_____

There are three types of beings:

- Those that have a beginning and an end _____

- Those that have a beginning but shall have no end _____
  _____

- One who has no beginning and no end _____

What kind of line would represent animals?_____

What kind of line would represent angels and men? _____

What kind of line would represent God? _____

The statement of eternality: _____

The significance of eternality:

- Torments of the lost are forever.

  - _____

  - _____

  - _____

- Rewards of the _____ are forever (1 Thess. 4:17).

- The _____ of the saved should be on eternity.

Student Work

Practical Uses of This Lesson

Knowledge of the eternality of God serves a believer no practical use unless he *meditates* upon and is *conscious* of these attributes. When one practices meditation, he gains the following benefits.

It Makes God Knowable and Predictable

A number of years ago, a man who had been held as a hostage in Iran and released, saw on television another hostage, who at the time was still in captivity. After watching the hostage interviewed, the former hostage said, "That's not the same man I knew when I was a hostage with him." What he meant was that the pressure of thirty–five days in captivity had changed the man. What he once was, he was no longer.

God is not like that. Once we discover what He was like three thousand years ago, we know what He is like today and what He will be like throughout the future.

Therefore, we must study His way with man through the centuries. For this reason, God recorded many of the historical incidents in the Old Testament. First Corinthians 10:1–11 describes the things that happened to Israel during the days of their wilderness wanderings. Verses 6 and 11 tell us why these events were recorded. Read the passage and state why they were recorded. _____

_____

This fact shows the importance of studying God! Therefore, when you read the stories of Israel—or of men such as David, Jeremiah, or Hezekiah—you should not study the *men* so much as you study the *God* of these men. Learn how God dealt with them, and you will know how He works today.

It Proves That We Are Saved Eternally

A God who never changes will never change His mind about our salvation. Since salvation is not based on how I act but entirely on what He did, I can rest assured that I am saved eternally. What does Ecclesiastes 3:14 say concerning this issue? _____

_____

_____

It Gives Eternal Values

Because God is eternal and His life is ours, we are eternal creatures. The old song says, "This world is not my home; I'm just a passing through." Therefore, we should live "with eternity's values in view."

Moses practiced this truth as recorded in Hebrews 11:24–26. How do we see Moses living with eternity's values in view in this passage?

_____

_____

_____

_____

_____

_____

The following chorus should be our daily prayer:

> With eternity's values in view, Lord;
> With eternity's values in view,
> May I do each day's work for Jesus
> With eternity's values in view.

If we could but "lay up for ourselves treasures in heaven" rather than on earth, how different would be our joys and blessings and how great an impact we could make on this earth for God.

Read Matthew 6:19–21. What is the folly of putting earthly things before heavenly (eternal) things? _____

_____

_____

This passage applies to more than money or material things. It also applies to things that occupy our attention, time, and energy. How often we spend our time, attention, and energy on things that soon pass away while neglecting things that will last for eternity.

In the following table, list examples of such things that will not count for eternity; then list examples of things that *will* count in eternity but that we often neglect in our lives in the opposite column.

Contrasting Things That Count and Things That Don't Count	
Passing things that do *not* count for eternity	Exercises and practices that do count for eternity but that we too often neglect

What do you plan to do about *your* values? Do you live with eternal things in mind, or do you live as though this life were all that mattered? Is your life so full of basketball, football, school work, dating or other social activities, etc., that you find that you hardly have time to pray, study your Bible, witness, or serve the Lord? Why not bow before your immutable, eternal God and confess your offense of living as though this world were your home?

Application Activities

1. Study the life of Hezekiah in 2 Kings 18–21 and record all of the ways in which God operates as seen in these chapters. Apply all of these ways to your life today by *showing what this means to you*. (Example: 2 Kings 18:7 shows that God honors those who honor Him. This means [to my life] that God will honor me if I give my life, as Hezekiah gave his, to honor Him.) In other words, don't study *Hezekiah* in these chapters; study *God* instead. Note *how* He thinks, and seek to discover the principles by which He operates. Note: This project comprises two parts: (a) recording the *ways* God operates and (b) recording *how* that affects your life.

2. Study 2 Kings 18–21, and record a providence of God as seen in the life of Hezekiah. Show how this providence is important to you today. Remember, the God of Hezekiah *never changes*. He is the same today!

3. Read *The Stars Speak* by Dr. Stewart Custer (bibliographic data are in the Recommended Reading List). Share (in writing or orally) some of the important biblical lessons we can learn from the study of astronomy. What do these astronomy lessons tell us about God?

4. Read and report on similar lessons learned from *The Earth, the Stars, and the Bible* by Paul M. Steidl (bibliographic data are in the Recommended Reading List).

CHAPTER 15

HIS IMMUTABILITY

"What [God] had decreed from eternity is unalterable. God's eternal counsel or decree is immutable."

—Thomas Watson, *A Body of Divinity*

In New Orleans in the summer of 1988, Vice President George Bush had just been nominated as the Republican candidate for the presidency. In his acceptance speech to the convention, he predicted that the Democrats in Congress would pressure him to raise taxes. He also predicted his inevitable response.

"They'll push me and pressure me. And I'll say to them, 'Read my lips: NO NEW TAXES!'"

The conventioneers erupted in cheers and thunderous applause. The media replayed that "read my lips" sound bite over and over throughout the next several months of the campaign. It played well with the voters, and Vice President Bush soon became President Bush.

In December, even before he was sworn into his new office, he met with his advisors at the vice–presidential residence to plan the policies of his new administration. There, in what his vice president Dan Quayle later termed "the pre–plummet summit," the president–elect succumbed to pressure from his own advisors to consider a tax hike in his negotiations with Congress.

He immediately began to get pounded by not only the media but also conservatives within his own party for breaking his most public promise. Although later in his administration he put together the largest military coalition since World War II, effectively expelling Saddam Hussein's Iraqi armies from Kuwait, he never recovered his image as a waffler and a promise breaker. In fact, *Time* magazine voted him the "Man of the Year" and featured *two* pictures of him on the cover: one showed a powerful, resolute Bush on the international scene, but the other showed a dim, weak, and vacillating Bush on domestic issues. In the end, the voters dealt him a crushing blow in his 1992 re–election bid and elected someone they thought they could trust to remain true to his word—Bill Clinton.

Clinton had presented himself as a "new Democrat." He pledged that his administration would be the most ethical administration in the history of the presidency. "The era of big government is over," he declared with finality. Then followed higher taxes, more government bureaucracy, intrusion into private life, personal moral scandals, impeachment, and massive foreign espionage.

Isn't *anyone* trustworthy? Can we take *anyone's* word?

Only one: God. He is "the same yesterday, and today, and forever" (Heb. 13:8). He "is not a man, that he should lie…" (Num. 23:19). When He says something, we can trust Him to mean it and to keep His word. "I am the Lord, I change not," He says (Mal. 3:6).

The doctrine of the eternality of God includes the fact that God never changes. If God ever changed, then He wouldn't be eternal, for to be eternal He must ever be the same. The fact of an unchanging God is called *immutability*. That is the attribute we study in this lesson.

Student Work

Initial Considerations

The word *immutable* means "unchanging." God does not change. He is always the same. This truth is closely tied to the eternality of God because, if God could change, He wouldn't be what He was before and thus would not be eternal.

Eternality implies immutability. What God was ten million years ago He is today. Therefore, the God of Abraham, Isaac, and Jacob is just the same today as He was in their day.

Read and put a circle around the five verses in the following list that best state the fact that God never changes or varies but is the same throughout the centuries.

Numbers 23:19	1 Samuel 15:29	Job 23:13
Psalm 33:11	Psalm 119:89	Proverbs 19:21
Ecclesiastes 3:14	Ecclesiastes 7:13	Isaiah 31:2
Isaiah 40:28	Isaiah 59:1	Hosea 13:14
Malachi 3:6	Romans 11:29	Hebrews 6:17
James 1:17	Psalm 102:27	Hebrews 13:8
John 8:57	2 Corinthians 1:20	Isaiah 14:24
2 Timothy 1:1	Hebrews 7:25	

An In–Depth Look at Immutability

Five things never change about the Lord. Let's take a closer look at these unchanging things.

God's Character Never Changes

God's love is always the same. He never loves us more at any one moment than He does at any other moment. Therefore, *I can do nothing to make Him love me more*. Likewise, His hatred of sin never changes. He treats sin now just as He has always treated it.

If God's character could change, then He would not be God because, if He changed, He would have to change either for better or for worse. If He changed for worse, then He would cease to be perfect, and if He changed for better, then He could not have been perfect before. Perfection implies that there can be no change.

God's Truth Never Changes

God's Word is eternal. He never changes His mind and rewrites His book. What He says shall stand eternally without the slightest alteration. What Scriptures state this fact? _____

God's Principles Never Change

God has laid down certain universal laws or principles by which He governs His universe. These principles cannot be violated successfully. A child of God is blessed and happy only when he or she discovers these principles and brings his or her life into full harmony with them.

God's Purpose Never Changes

Before God created the world, He devised a plan for man according to the counsel of His own will and good pleasure (Eph. 1). He has never altered that plan, nor will He ever deviate from it. God's purpose is as timeless as He.

God's Son Never Changes

God's Son is the same " _____

_____ " (Heb. 13:8). This fact is further proof of the deity of Jesus Christ. He has the same natural attributes as the Father. Only God can have such attributes; therefore, Jesus Christ is God.

Applications of This Doctrine

What do we learn from these five facts, and of what use are they to us? The following chart shows the benefits of God's immutability in the preceding five areas. Fill in the blanks in the chart using both the notes you took from the teacher's lesson and your own thoughts.

Benefits to the Believer of the Doctrine of Immutability	
God's Unchanging Characteristic	**Its Usefulness to the Believer**
1. God's character	I can trust His _____ . Because He never changes, I don't have to wonder or worry about His _____ . He isn't fickle. He will never turn on me. His love is always the same whether I please or displease Him. First Samuel 15:29 shows that He will not _____ _____ . How does this show that I can trust His Person and love? He will remain the same and not change His _____ or His _____ .
2. God's truth	I can trust His _____ . Whatever promises I discover in the Bible, He will fulfill. He has bound Himself to do what He says! What a glorious truth this is! How is this shown in James 1:17 and 2 Corinthians 1:20? With Him there is no variableness, neither _____ of turning. All of the _____ of God are sure in Christ.
3. God's ways	I can trust His _____ . God will not react to my actions any differently today than He did in Moses' day. Therefore, I can depend on what He will do. I can rely upon the principles I discover in the Bible. How is this shown in Malachi 3:6? He _____ that He _____ not.
4. God's purpose	I can trust His _____ . I never have to fear the news or the evil plots of mankind. Sovereign God is in control. His plan is eternal and cannot be thwarted or overturned. What He has determined, that He will do. Peace can thus be mine in the midst of turmoil, suffering, and persecution. How is this truth shown in Psalm 33:11; Isaiah 14:24; 46:10? God's counsel, thoughts stand _____ . As God has thought, purposed, so it will stand and come to pass. All of the promises of God are _____ in Christ.
5. God's Son	I can trust His _____ . Because His Son is always the same and my salvation rests with Him, I know that I have eternal life. The Son, who died for me, saved me, loves me, and keeps me, will never change His mind about me. He is always the same; therefore, my provision for heaven is sure. How is this truth shown in 2 Timothy 1:1? Christ is our _____ of life.

We have seen that the following five major uses of this great truth emerge from our discussion:

- His immutability gives me *security*.
- His immutability gives me *comfort*.
- His immutability gives me *faith*. I know that what He was in Bible times He still is today and that what He promises He will provide.
- His immutability gives me *stability*. I can plan, trust, make right decisions, and go to sleep in peace at night because I know His ways, His character, and His likes and dislikes.
- His immutability makes Him *knowable and predictable*.

Of course, we realize that we can never truly know God infinitely with our finite minds. However, we can come to know certain things about our God since He never changes. If He changed His mind, ways, moods, etc., we could never know Him. We would be at a loss to know how to please Him. We would be like a boat adrift with no compass or means of direction. But our God is predictable.

Therefore, it pays for us to study Him! The more we know of Him, the more we are able to please Him and to enjoy His unique person.

Do *you* study Him? Are *your* eyes fixed upon Him? Do *you* pursue Him with *your* thoughts?

"O, Lord, our Lord, How majestic is thy name!"

Notes from the Teacher's Lesson

God is _____ .

Immutability defined: _____
_____
_____ .

Characteristic	Use: I Can Trust His...	Scripture Reference
Character		James 1:17
Truth		Isaiah 40:8; Psalm 119:89
Ways		Malachi 3:6
Purposes		Isaiah 46:10
Son		Hebrews 13:8

Application Activities

1. Read 1 Samuel 15, and meditate on God's immutability as recorded in that passage. Write down the following things from the passage:

   • God's command to Saul
   • Saul's response to this command
   • The reason Saul disobeyed the command
   • What God desired most in Saul
   • What God thinks of rebellion and disobedience
   • God's punishment upon Saul
   • How God's unchanging character is seen in this passage
   • How God's unchanging truth is seen in this passage
   • How God's unchanging principles are seen in this passage
   • How God's unchanging purpose is seen in this passage

2. Meditate on God's immutability in His providences from the biblical category with the following situation: How David got to be king of Israel in place of Saul.

3. As we grow in the knowledge and grace of God, we are to become increasingly more like our Father. What implications does the doctrine of the immutability of God have for us in the following aspects of our lives:

   • Our character?
   • Our principles of life?
   • Our relationship to God's Son?
   • Our truthfulness?
   • Our purpose in life?

4. Read *The Power of Commitment* by Jerry White (bibliographic data are given in the Recommended Reading List). Describe the implications of God's expectations for us in becoming like Him in the following areas discussed in the book:

   - The lack of commitment in most people around us
   - Commitment in our spiritual walk
   - Commitment in the use of our material possessions and talents
   - Commitment in the use of our leisure time
   - Commitment and accountability
   - Commitment and family
   - The enemies of commitment

CHAPTER 16

HIS HOLINESS

"God is not only a pattern of holiness, but he is a principle of holiness: his spring feeds all our cisterns, he drops his holy oil of grace upon us."

—Thomas Watson, *A Body of Divinity*

In her book *Mission Possible*, Marilyn Laszlo tells of her experiences as a Wycliffe translator in the jungles of Papua New Guinea. The culture shock she experienced when she first arrived was almost unbearable. The people lived nonchalantly in extreme filth. They bathed along the banks of the same muddy river into which they threw their refuse and from which they drew their drinking water. They thought that clothing was for mere ornamentation. And they ate revolting foods.

The infrequent visitors Marilyn had from the United States always suffered the same culture shock when they arrived, and her sister Shirley was no exception. Marilyn relates how one day they were on a long hike to find an appropriate tree from which to carve a dugout canoe. Along the way, the natives presented the newly arrived Shirley with a leaf–packet and indicated by sign language that it was something for her to eat. She opened it and looked inside and then ran immediately to Marilyn.

"There's no way I can eat these!" she exclaimed in a loud whisper.

Marilyn looked inside the packet and saw several large steamed grubs, each the size of one's thumb. She had finally accustomed herself to eating the crunchy, roasted grubs that the natives frequently ate, but she had never eaten steamed grubs, which still looked fresh and juicy.

"But, Shirley, you *have* to eat them! You've only just arrived, and you don't want to offend them. They have honored you with this gift."

Shirley thought for a moment and then replied, "Okay, I'll try—but only if *you* eat one first!"

Marilyn tried to look casual as she popped one of the grubs into her mouth. It was too big to swallow whole, so she had to chew it. It was soft and squishy. She smiled at Shirley as she chewed. Shirley could see green grub juice beginning to trickle from the corners of Marilyn's mouth.

"Don't try them, Shirley!" Marilyn said quietly. "Let's just wrap them up and tell them we're taking them home to enjoy. It's a Sepik Iwam tradition."

Would you be repulsed if you had to live in such a culture? Of course you would! Then imagine the revulsion the holy Son of God must have felt when He left the holiness and purity of heaven and came to earth, taking upon Himself the body of a man and living among the filth of human sin and depravity. What love He had to do something so revolting to His holy sensibilities!

This lesson begins our study of the *moral* attributes of God. The first such attribute we'll study is His holiness.

Holiness is God's crown. This attribute has an excellency above His other attributes. Bible scholars agree that this doctrine is basic to the proper understanding of God and Christianity. If you would truly know God, you must understand His holiness; therefore, pay particular attention to the information in this lesson.

Student Work

The Importance of God's Holiness

God's Holiness Is Honored Above His Other Attributes

No Other Attribute Has a Triple Praise

- Read the following verses and then write out the triple declaration that both of them present: Isaiah 6:3 and Revelation 4:8—

  _____

- No other attribute is so honored. Nowhere does God say, "Eternal, eternal, eternal is the Lord God Almighty" or "Omniscient, omniscient, omniscient is the Lord." His holiness alone bears this honor.

This Is the Only Attribute by Which God Swears

Read Psalm 89:35. We see in this verse that God lays holiness to pledge for the assurance of His promise, as the attribute that is most dear to Him and most valued by Him. No one swears by that which he does not value. Therefore, God's supreme value of His holiness is seen in this unique statement.

His Holiness Is His Glory and Beauty

Stephen Charnock wrote, "Power is His hand and arm; omniscience, His eye (and brain); mercy, His bowels; eternity, His duration; but holiness is His beauty (2 Chron. 20:21)."

God's Holiness Is the Glory of All of His Other Attributes

Purity is the splendor of every attribute in the Godhead. His justice is a _holy_ justice; His omniscience is a _holy_ omniscience; His power is a _holy_ power (Ps. 98:1); and His promise is a _holy_ promise.

Imagine all of these perfections of God if they weren't holy! Without holiness, His patience would be an indulgence to sin. His mercy would become a fondness of sin, and His wrath would be a madness. Without holiness, His power would be a tyranny and His wisdom would be an unworthy subtlety.

Rather than describing God, who does the preceding paragraph describe? _____ Without two of God's attributes (holiness and infinity), you have created the Devil!

A Definition of Holiness

What is holiness? A study of the root word from which we translate our word *holy* will help us arrive at a good definition of *holiness*.

The Derivative of the Word Holiness

The Old Testament word for *holy* comes from the Hebrew root word *qdsh*, meaning "apartness, separateness." It comes from the root word *qd*, meaning "to cut."

The New Testament word for *holy* comes from the Greek word *hagios*, meaning "to set apart for a particular service."

The Two–Fold Definition

- Negatively—Holiness is separation *from* sin.
  - That which is holy cannot touch sin. What does Habakkuk 1:13 say about this point? _____
  _____
  _____

- Positively—Holiness is separation or separateness *to* God.
  - That is, whatever is holy is not only separated from sin but is also separate unto the glory and enjoyment of God. Charnock wrote, "Positively, holiness is a love for all truth, goodness, and righteousness."

Applying Holiness to God

Applying the preceding two–fold definition to God, we reach the following conclusions.

Negatively—God Is Absolutely Pure, Separate from and Incapable of Sin

Sin is like a magnet that pulls opposite to God's holiness. Therefore, when Christ took our sins on Himself on the cross, what did God do (Mark 15:34)? _____

_____

Read Psalm 22:1–3. What did Christ cry out while He was on the cross?

_____

_____

What answer do we find to this question in Psalm 22:1–3? _____

_____

From this we see that God cannot bear to look upon sin. Must it not have been an untold agony for Christ to live in the midst of a filthy and unholy people on this earth for thirty–three years? Everything about us was totally repugnant to the very nature of God.

Is it not an even greater wonder that God would *desire* to save us? There was nothing desirable about us. In fact, our whole fallen nature, our very being was nauseating to Him—because of His holiness.

Positively—God Has Set Himself Apart

According to Titus 2:14, God has set Himself apart for the purpose of

_____

_____.

_____

Applying Holiness to Christians

God's holiness has done—or does—several things.

God's Holiness Caused Him to Bar Man from Heaven (Rev. 21:27)

According to the preceding reference, what three things cannot enter heaven?

- _____
- _____
- _____

God, who cannot look on sin, could never let anything that is defiled by sin enter His holy presence. Therefore, only those who are pure and perfect can go to heaven.

God's Holiness Caused Him to Send Christ to Bear Our Sin

God, in His holiness, punished our sin by pouring out His wrath on His Son on the cross. Whatever is holy is healthy; sin brought death and corruption into the world. Therefore, a holy God moved to preserve His creation by destroying whatever would destroy His creation. Therefore, according to Hebrews 2:14, God sent His Son that He might "destroy

_____
_____."

Christ's death actually pleased God. Read Isaiah 53:10–12, where we see…

- what pleased the Lord— _____
  _____

- what satisfied the Lord—_____
  _____

- why He was so pleased and satisfied—_____
  _____
  _____

God's Holiness, When Man Sees It, Purifies Man's Life (Isa. 6:1–8)

Note the attribute of God that the angel mentions— _____

_____

What was the two–fold effect of this declaration on Isaiah?

- v. 5— _____

  _____

- v. 8— _____

  _____

God's Holiness Is the Basis for Personal Separation

What command do we have in 1 Peter 1:15–16? _____

_____

The *reason* we are to be (a) separated from sinful practices and (b) set apart for the service of God is rooted in the fact that we have a *holy* God.

Separation from Sin (Rom. 13:12–14)

- First, what are we to cast off? _____

  _____

- What specific sins are mentioned that must be destroyed?

  _____

  _____

- What does the phrase *make no provision for the flesh* mean?

  _____

  _____

Separation to God's Service (Rom. 12:1)

- On what basis is this request made? _____

  _____

- What is the *first* requirement mentioned for an acceptable sacrifice? _____

- God does not use unholy vessels. Second Timothy 2:22 bears this out. What three requirements are laid down in this verse for usefulness in God's service? _____

  _____

  _____

  _____

- Are you a fit vessel for the use of a holy God? May His holiness so grip our hearts and lives that we will give ourselves to Him with an undying dedication, and we will literally fear and hate sin. May God give us enough of His holiness to know some of His hatred and abhorrence of sin.

Application Activities

1. Explain the following statement: "There can be no worship, no spiritual growth, no true obedience without an understanding of God's holiness."

2. Why do you think that men are never really impressed with their own spiritual condition until they have contrasted themselves with the majestic holiness of God?

3. How is the holiness of God evident in the Exodus 14–15 account of the Israelites' crossing of the Red Sea and the destruction of the armies of Pharaoh when they tried to cross it too?

4. Read *Mission Possible* by Marilyn Laszlo (bibliographic data are given in the Recommended Reading List). Report on the lessons she learned about God's holiness while translating the Bible for the people of Papua New Guinea.

5. Read each of the verses in the following table. Then write in the middle column what the verse says about who you are in Christ. Then write in the right column the implied connection between your identity in Christ and the doctrine of holiness (i.e., your responsibility to be holy as God is holy).

Scripture Reference	In Christ, I Am...	Responsibility for Holiness
Matthew 5:13		
Matthew 5:14		
John 15:16		
1 Corinthians 3:16		
1 Corinthians 12:27		
2 Corinthians 5:18–19		
Ephesians 2:10		
Ephesians 2:19		
Ephesians 4:24		
1 Peter 2:5		
1 Peter 2:9–10		
1 Peter 2:11		

6. The following references deal with various aspects of God's holiness. Take time to read these verses as you delve deeper into the attribute of God's holiness. Write down the reference for each verse and then list the lessons that each of them teaches about God's holiness.

Exodus 3:5	Psalm 18:30	Isaiah 5:16	Habakkuk 1:12
Exodus 15:11	Psalm 22:3	Isaiah 6:3	Matthew 5:48
Leviticus 19:2	Psalm 30:4	Isaiah 12:6	Matthew 19:17
Deuteronomy 32:4	Isaiah 29:19	Luke 1:49	Joshua 24:19
Psalm 36:6	Isaiah 43:14	1 Samuel 2:2	Psalm 47:8
Isaiah 45:19	John 17:11	1 Samuel 6:20	Psalm 48:1
Isaiah 47:4	Romans 1:23	1 Chronicles 16:10	Psalm 60:6
Isaiah 49:7	Hebrews 1:8	Job 4:17	Psalm 89:35
Isaiah 52:10	James 1:13	Job 6:10	Psalm 92:15
Isaiah 57:15	1 Peter 1:15	Psalm 99:3	Jeremiah 2:5
1 John 1:5	Job 25:5	Psalm 111:9	Lamentations 3:38
1 John 2:20	Job 34:10	Psalm 119:142	Revelation 4:8
Job 36:23	Psalm 145:17	Revelation 6:10	Psalm 11:7
Proverbs 9:10	Hosea 11:9	Revelation 15:4	

CHAPTER 17

HIS JUSTICE AND RIGHTEOUSNESS

"God's justice is such that it is not fit for any man or angel to expostulate with him or demand a reason of his actions."

—Thomas Watson, *A Body of Divinity*

A man, his wife, and their daughter, who was home from a Christian college for the Christmas vacation, were on their way to church one dark, December Sunday night. Just as they rounded the curve at the top of a hill, another car came flying sideways over the hill from the other direction. The daughter, who was driving, had no time to react. The cars smashed together with a crunch of twisting metal, sending the mother into the windshield.

The man who was driving the other car received only minor injuries. Someone who lived in a nearby house heard the horrific collision and ran out in time to see him move from the driver's seat to the passenger side of the car. He later told police officers that a friend had been driving but had run from the accident scene, but the witness said that there had been no one else in the car. Officers found several recently emptied beer cans and liquor bottles on the floor of the car. Just from their conversation with him, they could tell that he was drunk. They confiscated his driver's license and took him to the hospital, where he was treated and released.

The mother in the other car, however, had life-threatening injuries. Her husband was also in critical condition, and her daughter was in guarded condition. As their mother lay in the intensive care unit in critical condition, the woman's two sons saw the policemen return the other driver's license as he left the hospital with hardly a scratch to show for the accident.

Two days later, the woman died, having never regained consciousness. Her husband, injured so badly that he couldn't attend her funeral, remained in the hospital for several more weeks. The daughter, who suffered the least injury, reluctantly and only at her father's urgent insistence, left him in the care of elderly relatives after the first of the new year and returned to resume her college studies.

The chief investigating officer dragged his feet on the case, and the sheriff refused to honor the victims' family members' request that he push for a speedy and thorough investigation and prosecution. A judge refused to issue an arrest warrant for the drunk driver, in spite of testimony by witnesses that he had bragged in a local bar about how he had killed a woman and walked off without any punishment.

Where was God in all of this? How could He allow such flagrant injustice to go unchecked and unpunished? How could a God who allowed such a travesty be called "loving"?

God *is* just. He *does* punish evil and wickedness. The problem is that we are impatient creatures. We want God to exact justice *now*.

But God doesn't always mete out His justice according to our timetable. As the timeless financiers' saying goes, "God doesn't settle all of His accounts in October." He's not constrained by anyone's fiscal year or calendar year. He has His own *perfect* timetable. Someone once said that the wheels of God's justice grind slowly, but they grind exceedingly fine.

Months passed following that family's tragic wreck. The daughter hobbled painfully around the campus attending her classes. The widower, a self–employed contractor, was out of work for nearly a year and without income. The other driver had no insurance, and the widower's own insurance company refused to pay out his claims. He had to take them to court to get his rightful payments.

Worst of all, he missed his wife of some thirty years sorely. He sought to escape the emotional pain and loneliness by immersing himself in the sixth–grade Sunday school class he and his wife had taught for many years. And he wrote letters to newspaper editors, community leaders, and elected officials, trying to increase public awareness of the tragedies of drunk driving. It was almost time for God to exact His justice.

The next year was an election year, and the sheriff was seeking re–election. His opponent ran a tough campaign; his primary issue was the need for tougher enforcement of drunk driving laws. The challenger won by a landslide. In one of his first acts of office, the new sheriff conducted a routine investigation of all department personnel. His investigation revealed that the officer who had refused to investigate the accident in our story had lied on his employment application. He fired him. A few months after the former sheriff left office, he was arrested, tried, convicted of masterminding a drug ring and a chop–shop operation (stealing and disassembling cars and then selling the parts illegally), and sentenced to prison. The drunk driver, who had bragged about having killed a woman and gotten away with it, committed suicide.

God *is* just. He is right in *everything* He does or allows to happen. We just have to trust His Word and wait patiently for Him to show His justice in *His* time. We have to believe that "all things work together for good to them that love God" (Rom. 8:28).

Notes from the Teacher's Lesson

God is _____.

God's justice and righteousness stated: _____

The significance of God's justice and righteousness:_____
_____
_____

Whereas *holiness* defines the character of God, *justice* (or righteousness) describes His character as expressed in his dealings with man. *Justice* in reference to God means that He is fair and honest and is not a respecter of persons.

Student Work

What do the following verses say about God's justice?

- Psalm 19:9— _____
  _____
  _____

- Psalm 145:17—_____
  _____
  _____

The most obvious application of God's justice is in His judgment of men. We have assurance that when God judges men they will get *exactly* what they deserve, exactly what is right. This knowledge is both a comfort and a terror. It comforts those who are ready, but it terrorizes those who are unprepared.

God's Truth About His Just Judgment

Read Acts 17:31, and answer the following questions.

- When will God judge the world? _____
  _____

- Who knows that day, month, and year? _____
  Therefore, *all* men should be prepared at *all* times.

- How will God judge the world? _____

- What does that mean? _____
  _____

- By whom will God judge the world? _____
  _____

That is, He will use Christ as the *standard* by which all men will be judged. Those who are not equal to Christ will be damned! Do you measure up to Christ? This is the idea in Romans 3:23: "For all have sinned and _____ of the glory of God."

Wherein do we fall short? (Examine the following illustration to find the answer to this question. Each of the answers is discussed in detail following the illustration.)

Perfect in:

- Holiness—Mark 1:24; Acts 3:14; Hebrews 7:26
- Justice—John 8:16
- Submission—John 8:29
- Speech—1 Peter 2:22
- Reactions—1 Peter 2:23
- Obedience—Philippians 2:5-8

(Look up the verses above in answering the following questions.)

We Fall Short of His Standard of Holiness

What do the demons admit of Christ? _____
_____

How did Peter describe Christ? _____
_____

According to Hebrews 7:26, how holy is Christ? _____
_____
_____

How close do you come to His perfect holiness? _____
_____
_____

We Fall Short of His Standard of Justice

How does Jesus describe His own judgment? _____

Are you that perfect in your judgment of people and circumstances? Do you always see things *exactly* as they are? Are you ever fooled by anything or anyone? Christ was *never* wrong! He *never* misjudged anyone's actions, character, or motives.

We Fall Short of His Standard of Submission

How submissive was He? _____

_____

How close to that standard do *you* come? _____

_____

_____

We Fall Short of His Standard of Speech

What was true of Christ's speech? _____

_____

Can this be said of us? _____

We Fall Short of His Standard in Our Reactions to Mistreatment

How did Christ react to mistreatment? _____

_____

_____

_____

How would *you* have reacted, based on how you react now when someone attacks you unjustly? _____

_____

_____

We Fall Short of His Standard of Obedience

How obedient was Christ? _____

_____

Can we say that we are even close to perfect obedience to His Word?

_____

Remember: *God will judge man by this perfect standard!*

What is God's guarantee that He will judge the world by Christ's standard? _____

If God were to judge your soul today for heaven or hell, based on whether you measured up to Christ's standard, where would you go? That is exactly how God judges every man!

Man's Doubts About God's Judgment

Perhaps you've had a nagging doubt concerning God's justice. Some men wonder if God can save a sinner and still be just. In other words, if man must be absolutely as perfect as Christ to go to heaven, how can *any* man make it (for "all have sinned and *come short* of the glory of God")? The answer is found in Christ and Christ alone.

I fall short of God's righteous requirements (Rom. 3:23).

I can do nothing to meet His demands. How does Romans 8:8 express this fact? _____

_____

Christ took my place by…

- Fulfilling God's requirements with a perfect life

- Paying the penalty for my sin by His shed blood

- How does Romans 5:10 express these facts? _____

  _____

  _____

  _____

Thus, when I accept Christ, He *becomes* my righteousness (1 Cor. 1:30) and His righteousness is *imputed* (charged) to my account (Rom. 4:6, 11, 23–24).

Thus, when God sees me, He sees not my sin but Christ's perfections. Therefore, we are "_____ (by God) in the _____" [Christ] (Eph. 1:6).

Therefore, God can be *just* when He justifies a sinner and declares him to be righteous (Rom. 3:26).

Application Activities

1. Read and meditate on Romans 2:1–16. List all of the things you see in that passage about the justice of God in dealing with men.

2. Meditate on the justice of God in His providences. Record a providence (in any category) that displays the justice of God in His dealings with men.

3. Memorize and meditate on Jeremiah 9:24.

4. List personal problems or injustices that you are praying for God to resolve. Continue praying that you might see His justice and righteousness displayed in those matters, but pray also for the patience to wait for His timing and not succumb to the temptation to take matters into your own hands.

5. Someone has said, "God will not do for me what I can do for myself, but He will not let me do for myself what only He can do." Conduct a Bible study to determine how to discern when one should continue simply to pray and to wait patiently for God to act and when he should take action himself.

6. Share a story (perhaps the story at the beginning of this chapter will spur your memory) in which an injustice was righted in God's timing and in an unlikely way. What lessons did you (or can we) learn from that incident?

Isaiah 49:16 SEE I have Engraved
William Sarah
Michelle Amanda Matthew
George Adam
Joseph
Louis Jack Mary
Tamika Carol Luke
Owen
Katie Curtis Clifton Nicholas Tim
Mark Jim
Paula Jean Samuel
Nicole Kedra
Phillip Selena Jessika
Eugenia Mike Andrew Gilda
Adele Scott Aeden Delores Rae
Selim Anson Abby Cole Nyasha Kim
Lisa Kennedy Theresa Julia Hanna
Keith Gretchen Gayle Martha
Austin Mitchell Cedric
Leah Irma Bobby
David Nora Josiah

CHAPTER 18

HIS MERCY AND GRACE

"Of all God's attributes, mercy is the crown."

—Andrew Murray, *God's Best Secrets*

Frederick William Faber penned the following words of a hymn in 1854:

> There's a wideness in God's mercy,
> Like a wideness of the sea;
> There's a kindness in His justice,
> Which is more than liberty.

The hymn's message is still as true and powerful today as it was on that day. He surely was moved and impressed by that message, and he wanted to share with others the great depths of that crowning attribute of God's mercy for he wrote a total of twelve verses to the hymn.

The musical score for the poem was written by Lizzie Shove Tourjée Estabrook in 1878 for her high school graduation. Lizzie was the daughter of Eben Tourjée, founder of the New England Conservatory of Music.

The "meat" of the hymn, however, is its application of God's mercy to those who deserve it least—sinners. After all, mercy is by definition something offered to those who do not deserve it. This message is clear in the following verse. May you, the student, grow to recognize the breadth and depth of God's mercy as you study this lesson.

There is welcome for the sinner,
And more graces for the good;
There is mercy with the Savior;
There is healing in His blood.

We enjoy God's mercies afresh every morning, and He abundantly showers mercies upon us throughout the day. He is merciful to us even in our sleep.

We also enjoy God's grace daily. How badly we deserve His justice, but He withholds it in love and gives us mercies instead. Knowing this fact should make us want to sing the following words from Thomas O. Chisholm's famous hymn:

Great is Thy faithfulness!
Morning by morning new mercies I see;
All I have needed Thy hand hath provided—
Great is Thy faithfulness, Lord, unto me!

Notes from the Teacher's Lesson

God is _____.

God's mercy and grace defined:

- Mercy—_____
  _____

- Grace— _____
  _____

God's mercy and grace stated: _____

The significance of God's mercy and grace: _____
_____
_____
_____

From Matthew 18:21–35, we learn about the following two things:

- God's mercy and grace to us (vv. 21–27)
- Our mercy and grace to others (vv. 28–35)

Compared to our offenses against God, offenses against us are as a drop of water in the ocean.

It is not possible for anyone to commit an offense against us greater than any offense we have committed against God.

From this text we also see the following progression:

- The debt is _____ .
- The debt is _____ .
- The debtor is _____ .

How to Forgive

The key to forgiveness is _____

_____ .

- _____
- _____
- _____
- _____
  - _____
  - _____
  - _____
  - _____
- _____
  _____

Student Work

Mercy Examined

Mercy and Grace

Grace is receiving something good that you don't deserve. Mercy is not receiving bad that you do deserve. Therefore, grace has to do with heaven whereas mercy has to do with hell. Through mercy we are saved from hell; through grace we are saved for heaven.

Mercy and Goodness

Mercy is the result *and* the effect of God's goodness (Ps. 23:6). Because God is good, He is merciful.

Mercy Is God's Glory (Exo. 33:18–19)

What did Moses ask to see? _____

What three things did God tell Moses He would show him?

- _____
- _____
- _____

These three things are considered to be God's glory!

God's glory shines no brighter than when He bends to sweeten sorrow or stay His wrath. It is God's glory to save us from hell.

God's Mercy Is Free

Nothing can deserve mercy, for if we deserved it, it wouldn't be merciful. Like grace, it must be free (and thus undeserved).

- _____ is free (Rom. 3:24).
- _____ is free (Titus 3:5).
- _____ are free (Rom. 8:32).
- _____ is free (Rev. 22:17).

God's Mercy Is Infinite

There are no bounds or limits to God's free mercy. His mercy is…

- _____ (Ps. 86:5)
- _____ (Eph. 2:4)
- _____ (Lam. 3:23)

God's Mercy Is Eternal

His mercy is from _____
(Ps. 103:17). How many times do we learn of the eternality of His mercy
in Psalm 136? _____

As long as He is God, there will be mercy. If we could remember that
God's mercy is not a temporary mood but an attribute of God's eternal
being, we would no longer fear that it will sometimes cease to be. His
mercy stands forever—night and day, asleep or awake.

All Mercy Is Derived from God

What title is given to God the Father in 2 Corinthians 1:3? _____
_____ He is called this because
He begets all of the mercies in the world.

God's Greatest Mercy Is Found in Christ

Read Leviticus 26:4–6, 12. List all of the blessings that God promises
Israel in these verses. _____

_____

_____

_____

_____

_____

_____

_____

Of these mercies, which is the greatest? _____

To have health is a mercy, but to have Christ and salvation is a greater mercy. Of all the things we deserve, we deserve hell most. Therefore, to have salvation from hell through Christ is the greatest mercy available to man today.

Application Activities

1. Read and meditate on God's mercies in Psalm 136. Record all of the things you see about God's mercy as it is manifested in the following aspects of God:

   - His person (vv. 1–3) – three things
   - His power (vv. 4–9) – six things
   - His past history (vv. 10–24) – eleven things
   - His providences (v. 25) – one thing

2. Read and meditate on God's providences in Psalm 103. Cite a providence either in your life or that of a contemporary in which God gave mercy when wrath was deserved. From the psalm, answer the following questions.

   - What are we not to forget?
   - What is a Christian's crown?
   - How does His mercy relate to our sinfulness in verse 10?
   - What if He dealt with us according to our sin?
   - How great is His mercy?
   - To whom is His mercy offered?
   - According to verse 12, how does His mercy relate to sin?
   - How long will His mercy endure?

3. Think of someone who has wronged you in some way. (Maybe they said something hurtful about you, damaged something that belonged to you, misrepresented something you did or said, etc.) Following the steps outlined in this lesson, seek their forgiveness. Record the steps you take and the results obtained.

4. Read Charles Haddon Spurgeon's little book *All of Grace*. Summarize the lessons learned from your reading. Include pertinent quotations

from the book in your summary. List the examples of God's grace that he includes.

5. Make a list of people who have been gracious to you. Beside their names write a brief description of their gracious actions. Next, make a list of people to whom you can be gracious (focus on people to whom others tend not to be kind). Write down practical ways in which you can be gracious to them. Then do it!

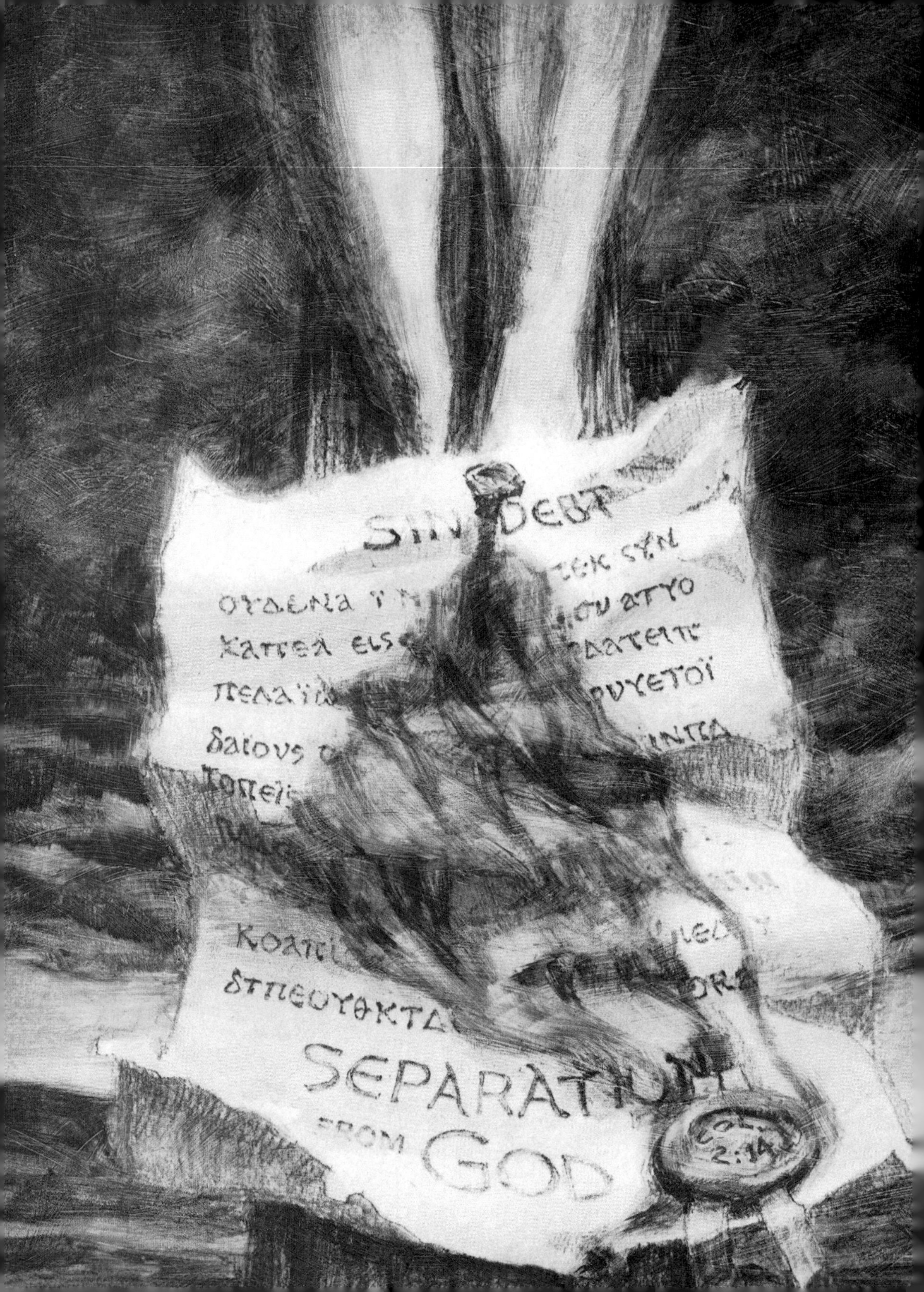
SIN DEBT
SEPARATION
FROM GOD
COL. 2:14

CHAPTER 19

HIS LOVE

"All the other attributes of God…find in [God's love] their highest glory."
—Andrew Murray, *God's Best Secrets*

Frederick Martin Lehman sat down in 1919 and wrote a hymn that summarizes the central message of the attribute discussed in this lesson—the love of God. Even as the love of God has its beginning in eternity past, the words and tune of this hymn have a long history and an international flavor.

Lehman adapted the words to his hymn from a Jewish poem, *Hadamut*, which was written in Aramaic in 1050 by Meir Ben Isaac Nehorai of Worms, Germany. Lehman's daughter, Claudia Lehman Mays, arranged the music.

Even as the words and music of the hymn have a wide geographic flavor in their history, so God's love is eternal and reaches to all peoples, nations, and tongues. The message of its words reaches beyond all boundaries to the hearts of sinful men, convicting them of sin, and of Christians, comforting them and offering them hope for both the present and the future.

> The love of God is greater far
> Than tongue or pen can ever tell;
> It goes beyond the highest star,
> And reaches to the lowest hell.
> The guilty pair, bowed down with care,

God gave His Son to win;
His erring child He reconciled,
And pardoned from his sin.

When years of time shall pass away,
And earthly thrones and kingdoms fall,
When men, who here refuse to pray,
On rocks and hills and mountains call,
God's love so sure, shall still endure,
All measureless and strong;
Redeeming grace to Adam's race—
The saints' and angels' song.

Could we with ink the ocean fill,
And were the skies of parchment made,
Were every stalk on earth a quill,
And every man a scribe by trade,
To write the love of God above,
Would drain the ocean dry.
Nor could the scroll contain the whole,
Though stretched from sky to sky.

Trying to describe or define the love of God is like an ant's trying to describe a mountain using his own world as a reference point. God's love is so great and majestic that man finds himself totally inadequate even to begin to fathom it, much less describe it. The preceding hymn clearly states the difficulties of so describing God's love.

O love of God, how rich and pure!
How measureless and strong!
It shall for evermore endure
The saints' and angels' song.

A. W. Tozer said, "I can no more do justice to that awesome and wonder–filled theme [the love of God] than a child can grasp a star. Still, by reaching toward the star the child may call attention to it."

Thus, with a sense of awe and inadequacy, we draw our attention to this vast, incomprehensible attribute of God.

Notes from the Teacher's Lesson

Defined:

Love— _____

_____

_____

God's love—that in God _____

_____

spontaneously, voluntarily, and righteously for the_____

of personal beings regardless of their _____

_____ .

Types of Love Man Experiences

• _____

• _____

• _____

• _____

God's love stated: _____

• _____ of love (v. 7)

• _____ of love (v. 8)

• _____ of God's love (vv. 9–10)

  • Through _____

  • To _____

  • Towards _____

On the following table, show how each of the attributes of God further
defines His love by writing what effect that attribute has on His love.

God's Attributes as Definers of His Love	
Attribute	**Effect on His Love**
Self–existence	Has no _____ _____ _____ _____
Eternality	Has no _____
Justice/righteousness	Is _____ (Love doesn't get in the way of doing what is right. For example, teens may allow a date to keep them out of church.)
Infinity	Is _____ (He proved this by stooping to the lowest depths to obtain our salvation.)
Holiness	Is _____ (not based on lust and selfishness)
Omniscience, omnipresence, omnipotence, immensity)	Is incomprehensibly _____
Mercy/grace	Is without human _____ _____
Immutability	_____ (is not fickle or moody)

The significance of God's love: _____

- _____ (v. 10)

- _____ (v. 11)

- _____ (vv. 17–18)

Student Work

Our Love to Him

One cannot study God's love to man without soon becoming aware that His own love to God is pitiful and weak. In fact, God's love and man's love are not even of the same type. We have noted that God loved an object that was not lovable. That is, there was nothing about the object that caused God to love it. God had to *will* to love us. He loved us by *choice*.

Man cannot love as God loves. We humans must have a *reason* to love. There must be something lovable in the objects we love. Therefore, when one beholds the beauties, glories, and graces of God, is there any question that He should be the most loved object in all the universe?

The Basis of Our Love to Him

To love Him, we must know Him. This point reminds us of our master chart from lesson 2. God's love for us is seen in that He desires His will for us and planned how that will would be accomplished. His Son then provided the means for obtaining that will by dying on Calvary's cross. His Spirit then empowered us to accomplish that will.

God has done all that He will do. At this point, human responsibility enters the picture. To do that will, we must (a) *be* and *do* holiness. But before we will be holy and practice holiness, we must (b) love Him. Yet, we cannot love Him if we do not (c) know Him.

Thomas Watson wrote, "The antecedent of love is knowledge. The Spirit shines upon the understanding [as we meditate on His Word and providences], and discovers the beauties of wisdom, holiness, and mercy in God; and these are the loadstone to entice and draw out love to God. Such as know not God cannot love him; if the sun be set in the understanding, there must needs be night in the affections."

The Nature of Our Love to Him

The nature of love consists in delighting in an object. Thus, we learn from Psalm 37:4, we are to _____

_____

as a bride delights in her new–found love.

The Quality of Our Love to Him

It is not enough to say, "I love God." Such a being as our immaculate, majestic God must be loved with a quality that outstrips our love for anything or anyone else. Note the following qualities that are found in sincere love to God.

We Love God _____ (Matt. 22:37)

> God would have our whole heart. We must not divide our love between Him and sin. It is beneath His dignity to share any part of His heart with earthly objects. This is one reason idolatry is such a hated sin.

We Love God with All of Our Heart, Soul, and _____ (Deut. 6:5)

> The Hebrew word for *love* indicates vehemence. In other words, we must love God as much as we are able. We should be as the cherubim of Ezekiel, blazing in holy love. We can never love God as much as He deserves.

We Love God for Himself (Ps. 18:1)

> "I will _____, O Lord, my _____." We must love God for what He is in Himself—for His excellencies, for His loveliness. Hypocrites love God because He gives them corn and wine; we must love Him for Himself, for those shining perfections which are in Him.

We Must Love God _____ for Him (1 Thess. 1:3)

> Love is active and industrious in nature; it sets the head studying for God, the hands working, and the feet running in the _____

_____ (Ps. 119:32).
This is called a _____
in 1 Thessalonians 1:3. Mary Magdalene loved Christ and _____
_____ on Him (John 12:3).
We can never do enough for Him whom we love.

We Must Love God Preeminently

God is the essence of beauty, a whole paradise of delight, and He must have a priority in our love. "We may give the creature the milk of our love, but God must have the cream" (Thomas Watson).

We Must Love God Constantly

"_____ cannot quench love, neither can the _____ drown it" (Song of Sol. 8:7). The floodwaters of persecution can never dampen a sincere love for God. According to Ephesians 3:17, we should be _____ _____ in love. A branch withers that does not grow on a root; so love deeply rooted in the glories of God will stand the trials of time.

The Visible Signs of Our Love to Him

If we truly love Him, seven signs of our love will be visible.

Our Desire Will Be After Him

"The _____ of our soul is to _____ _____" (Isa. 26:8). Again, "My soul _____ for _____, for the _____ _____" (Ps. 42:2). He who loves God desires to be much in His presence; he loves to be in God's house and to fellowship with Him through songs and the hearing of the Word.

We Cannot Find Contentment in Anything Without Him

A gracious soul can do without health, but it cannot do without God, who is the _____

_____

(Ps. 43:5). If God should say to a soul that entirely loves Him, "Take thy ease, swim in pleasure, enjoy the delights of the world; but thou shalt not have my presence," this would not content that soul. If God should say, "I will let thee be taken up to heaven, but I will retire into another room, and thou shalt not see my face," it would not content the soul. It is hell to be without God! (Note that the ultimate torment of Hell will be the soul's eternal separation from God.)

We Grieve over That Which Grieves Him

If we have true love in our heart to God, we cannot but grieve over those things that grieve Him. Our heart will be as David's, who said, " _____

_____ because they _____" (Ps. 119:136). Again, David's attitude toward the sinful practices of others is reflected in Psalm 119:53: " _____

_____ because of the _____ who _____

_____." Some people speak of the sins of others and laugh at them, but they surely have no love to God who can laugh at that which grieves His Spirit!

We Weep Bitterly When He Is Absent

Thus did _____ (John 20:13). One cries, "My health is gone!" Another cries, "My estate is gone!" But he who is a lover of God cries out, "My God is gone! I cannot enjoy Him whom I love." If we mourn the loss of a loved one, much more should we weep over the loss of His sweet presence. Such a soul pours forth floods of tears and seems to say, "Lord, thou art in heaven, hearing the melodious songs of angels; but I sit here in the valley of tears, weeping because I have lost thy presence. Oh, when wilt thou come to me, and revive me with the light of thy countenance? Or, Lord, if thou wilt not come to me, let me come to thee, where I shall have the perpetual smile of thy face in heaven." Do you have His presence? Do you long for it?

We Labor to Make Him Lovely to Others

He who admires God speaks of His praises that he may allure and draw others to be in love with Him. True love cannot be silent but will be eloquent in setting forth His renown. *There is no better sign of loving God than to make Him appear lovely and to draw others to Him.*

We Will Be Willing to Do And Suffer for Him

First Corinthians 13:7 explains, "Love beareth all things, believeth all things, hopeth all things, _____ _____." Love made Christ suffer for us, and love will make us willing to suffer for Him. Although not every Christian is a martyr, every Christian has a spirit of martyrdom in him. Thus, he is as Paul, "_____to be ____ _____" (2 Tim. 4:6). Many people say that they love God, but they will not suffer the loss of anything for Him. What if Christ has said, "I love you well, but I cannot suffer for you, I cannot die for you"? Should we not have then questioned His love, and may not the Lord question ours, when we pretend love to Him, but will not endure the loss of any possession or pleasure for His sake?

Challenge

Love is the heart of Christianity; it is the grace after which Christ most inquires. "Simon, son of Jonas," Jesus asked, "_____ _____ " (John 21:15). Is it a hard request to love God? Was ever a debt easier to pay than this?

Nothing else under heaven deserves our love! Reserve all of your love for Him.

Application Activities

1. Read and study 1 Corinthians 13, the "love chapter." Make a list of all of the characteristics of love found in that chapter. Beside each characteristic, write one practical application that a teenager can make in his home of that characteristic.

2. Using the example of Christ and the characteristics listed in 1 Corinthians 13, write a paper describing how God's love is to be the pattern for a husband's (boys) or a wife's (girls) love for his or her spouse.

3. Read carefully the following excerpt from William Shakespeare's *Sonnet 116*. Then select *one* of the four underlined portions (three portions of two lines each and one one–line portion) and write a paper explaining it in light of God's love.

    > …Love is not love
    > Which alters when it alteration finds,
    > Or bends with the remover to remove:
    > O, no! it is an ever–fixed mark,
    > That looks on tempests and is never shaken
    > It is the star to every wandering bark,
    > Whose worth's unknown, although his height be taken.
    > Love's not Time's fool, though rosy lips and cheeks
    > Within his bending sickle's compass come;
    > Love alters not with his brief hours and weeks
    > But bears it out even to the edge of doom.

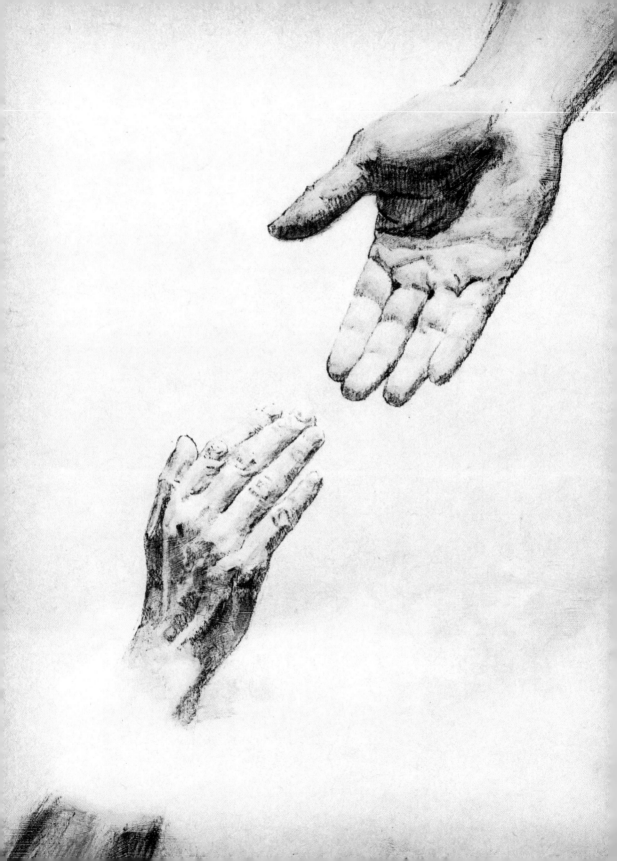

CHAPTER 20

KNOWING GOD: A REVIEW

"It is little comfort to know there is a God, unless He be ours. God offers Himself to be our God. And faith catches hold of the offer, it appropriates God, and makes all that is in Him over to us to be ours: His wisdom to be ours, to teach us; His holiness ours, to sanctify us; His Spirit ours, to comfort us; His mercy ours, to save us."

—Thomas Watson, *A Body of Divinity*

This chapter is designed to offer you help in preparing for Unit Test 3. Unit 3 is long and contains information that is deep and sometimes hard to be understood, so you will benefit from the extra review before you attempt to take the unit test.

Your teacher's lesson (including the following notes that you should take from that lesson) will guide your review of the nature and the natural and moral attributes of God. Your teacher may also go beyond the review given in the teacher's materials and provide additional review material.

The teacher will also try to establish firmly in your mind—not only for the test but also for life to come—the principles covered in Unit 3. He or she will also challenge you to give your life to the God whose attributes you have been studying during this unit.

Notes from the Teacher's Lesson

God's _____—"I am the Lord" (Exo. 20:1–3)

Lord = _____

God's _____

God's _____

God's _____

_____

God's _____—"Thy God"

God = Elohim—faithfulness to keep His covenant and promises to His people.

God is our _____

God's _____—"Thy God"

What Are the Means?

- Man is _____
  _____ .

- Man must _____
  _____ .

- A substitute was _____
  _____ .

- All who _____
  _____ .

What Are the Blessings?

- We feel the _____ of evil but not the
  _____.

- Our _____ .

- He _____ .

- He does more for us than the _____ .

- _____

- _____

Student Work

Practice Test

Following is a practice test to help you prepare for the regular unit test. Your teacher may assign this as an in–class activity, a small–group activity, or an open–book take–home test. Regardless of how it is assigned, put it to good use in reviewing the materials covered in chapters 11–19. You can use your previous outlines or class notes to answer the questions. Although most of the questions are given here as short answer–type questions or fill–in–the–blank questions, the regular unit test will consist of a variety of question types, including true–false, multiple choice, matching, short answer, and essay items. You should be prepared to find the information from chapters 11–19 in all of these types of questions.

1. On what three fundamental facts are all schools of learning based?

   - _____
     _____

   - _____
     _____

   - _____
     _____

2. State how man's chief end is accomplished by completing the following sentences.

- God _____ how we would glorify Him.

- Christ _____ the way.

- The Holy Spirit _____ it in us.

- As we _____ on _____ in the _____ and in _____ we come to _____ Him.

- As we get to know God, we come to _____ Him, which, in turn, causes us to _____ and to _____ things/actions. Thus, we come to glorify Him.

3. Why is it important that we focus on the right thing in God's Word?

_____

_____

_____

_____

4. On what must we focus in the Word? _____

_____

5. Name two things that knowing God is *not*.

- _____

- _____

6. Knowing God involves what two things?

- _____

- _____

7. How does one turn knowledge *about* God into knowledge *of* God (two steps)?

   • _____

   • _____

8. What is the four–fold definition of *providences*?

   • _____

   • _____

   • For our own good and His glory

   • _____

9. What are the four main steps necessary in meditating on God's providences?

   • _____

   • _____

   • Ponder the timeliness, leading edge, instrument used, and Scriptures

   • And the most important step: _____
     _____
     _____

10. Name *in order* (beginning with the *most* important) a Christian's three priorities.

   • _____

   • _____

   • _____

11. What is a life message? _____
   _____
   _____

12. How is one's ministry broadened? _____

_____

13. What is the secret to meditation? _____

_____

14. For what four reasons must we know what God is like?

- _____

- _____

- _____

- _____

15. What is God's essence? _____

_____

How does this differ from His attributes? _____

_____

16. What are four major uses of the doctrine of the Trinity?

- _____

- _____

- _____

- _____

17. Which attribute of God…

- Is seen in the name *El Shaddai*? _____

- Is seen in the word *La Hai Roi*? _____

- Causes us to let God make our decisions? _____

- Is stated in John 4:7–10? _____

- Is the attribute that God honors above all others? _____

- Produces faith when you are misunderstood? _____

- Is the basis for personal separation? _____

- Is stated in Exodus 34:6? _____

- Makes God knowable and predictable? _____

18. What is the two–fold definition of *holiness*?

- Negative: _____
  _____

- Positive: _____
  _____

19. What is mercy? _____
_____

20. What are the five steps to obtaining the forgiveness of someone we have offended?

- _____
  _____

- _____
  _____

- _____
  _____

- _____
  _____

- _____
  _____

21. Which kind of love is each of the following?

- Based on emotions _____

- Based on physical, mental, and emotional affinity _____
  _____

- Based on the physical _____

- True love _____

22. Name seven signs that one loves God.

- _____

- _____

- _____

- _____

- _____

- _____

- _____

23. Finish the following sentence: Nothing under heaven deserves _____
_____
_____

24. What basic difference between man's love and God's love is seen in 1 John 4:19? _____
_____
_____

25. Which lesson in this unit meant the most to you personally and why?_____
_____
_____
_____
_____
_____
_____
_____
_____
_____

UNIT 4

THE HISTORY OF CHRIST

"If Jesus Christ was so abased for us, took our flesh, which was a disparagement to Him, mingling dust with gold, if He abased Himself so for us, let us be willing to be abased for Him."

—Thomas Watson, *A Body of Divinity*

CHAPTER 21

THE PRECIOUSNESS OF CHRIST

"[Fullness of grace] no saint on earth has; he may excel in one grace, but not in all; as Abraham was eminent for faith, Moses for meekness; but Christ excels in every grace."

—Thomas Watson, *A Body of Divinity*

The British take matters of their royalty very seriously. It doesn't seem to matter to them that their monarch is actually nothing more than a symbol, a mere figurehead of past glories, or that the crown actually does nothing in running their government. They are content to pay high taxes to keep the royal family living in a manner befitting royalty.

Perhaps the greatest symbol of the monarchy is the Crown Jewels. According to the royal family's official web page, the value of the Crown Jewels "represents more than gold and precious stones. The Crown Jewels are part of the national heritage and held by The Queen as Sovereign." They (or some parts of them) have been used by English kings and queens since the days of King John or earlier. Today, however, they are used only rarely, and that only on very, very special occasions. The rest of the time, they are kept under extremely close security. And considering how they were treated earlier in the monarchy, one can understand why.

King John (he of *Magna Carta* infamy) is said to have lost them in quick-sand in 1216. Edward III pawned them to pay his troops, who were fighting for him overseas. (After they were retrieved, the pawning practice was forbidden—but Charles I's queen still managed to pawn them in Holland at the beginning of the English Civil War.) Oliver Cromwell detested the monarchy and ordered them to "'be totally broken; as being symbolic of the 'detestable rule of kings.'" The jewels were sold separately, but the Crown Jewels were reassembled when the monarchy was restored. Since that time, many additions have been made to the Crown Jewel collection.

Ever since a theft of the Crown Jewels in 1303 (they obviously were retrieved), they have been housed in the Tower of London. At first, they were merely kept in a locked cupboard in the days of Charles II. After they were nearly stolen again, an armed guard was added. In the 1700s, curious visitors had to be willing to be locked into a windowless room with a very vigilant armed guard and to be content to look at them from their seats if they wanted to view the Crown Jewels. The jewels were later placed on turntables in glass cases behind a rail for better viewing. A new Jewel House was opened in 1868, and the jewels remained there for about a hundred years. During World War II, the Crown Jewels were secreted away to who knows where and then returned to London at the end of the war.

The British built an underground Jewel House in 1967, but it could not cope with the approximately 15,000 people a day who wanted to see the Crown Jewels. The most recent Jewel House was opened in 1994, again at the Tower of London, and this time with unspecified "additional technology" for their security.

To the British, these jewels are indeed precious. Not only are they costly in themselves but also the British government and people are willing to go to great lengths and expenses to preserve, protect, and defend these symbols of the British heritage. They are rightfully proud of them; therefore, they try to make them highly valued among not only their own citizens but also the people of the entire world.

Believers also have a Crown Jewel. It is our Lord and Savior Jesus Christ. In comparison to the value the British place on their earthly Crown Jewels, how highly do you value the heavenly Crown Jewel? To what lengths of effort, expense, and sacrifice are you willing to go on His behalf? Do you keep Him hidden away for only occasional use or viewing by curious visitors, or are you presenting Him publicly? Are you willing to offer your life as a living sacrifice in order to make Him attractive to a sin–cursed world?

We begin our study of Christ, the second person of the Godhead, by considering His value. First Peter 2:7 says that He is "precious," using the word in the sense in which we use it when we speak of precious jewels. The word is actually *costly* or *expensive*. Sometimes we refer to something as "priceless." This is the true Christian's estimate of the person of Christ.

In this lesson, we are discussing a subject of the highest and most excellent value. We should approach it with a sense of awe and respect. Prayerfully ascend the steps of this lesson; we are entering the very throne room of our Lord and Savior Jesus Christ.

Notes from the Teacher's Lesson

God's Greatest _____ (John 21:15)

It is not what you do or know; it is what you are.

God's Greatest _____ (Eph. 6:23–24)

Grace

God's Riches At Christ's Expense

- _____
- _____
- _____

Love

Peace

Faith

Our Natural _____ **(1 Pet. 2:7–8)**

He Is Not Precious to…

• _____

• _____

He Is Precious to…

• The _____
    • All the doctrines center in Christ.
    • All the graces and comforts of a Christian reside in Him.
    • All the fullness of the Godhead dwells bodily in Him.

• _____

Application Activities

1. Memorize 1 Peter 2:7.

2. Meditate on Christ. In preparation for your meditation time, read John 1 slowly and carefully. Then think about Christ for thirty minutes, thanking God for Him and for what you learn of Him from John 1. Then write a paper titled "What Christ Means to Me." Share the paper with the class.

3. Record a providence (any category) in which you found the presence and/or power of Christ very important.

4. Access the web and locate the coronation script for the coronation of Queen Elizabeth in 1953 (the official web page of the British Monarchy [www.royal.gov.uk/] is a good place to start). As you read through the program (it lists what every participant, including the audience, is to do and say), take special note of how many religious references were included. (Examples include hymns, Scripture readings, creed recitations, references to and veneration of the Bible, etc.) Contrast these visible outward signs of Christianity with the realities of declining Christian influence in daily life in Great Britain today.

5. Read chapter 1 ("Seeing Christ's Glory") of *The Glory of Christ* by John Owen. (Bibliographic data are included in the Recommended Reading List.) Note particularly the four rewards listed for those who are willing to study the glory and preciousness of Christ.

C H A P T E R   2 2

THE PRE—EXISTENCE OF CHRIST

"In the beginning was the word, and the word was with God, and the word was God. And the word was made flesh, and dwelt among us, (and we beheld his glory, the glory as of the only begotten of the Father) full of grace and truth."

—John 1:1, 14

Imagine that you are talking with someone whom you assume, based on his outward appearance, is about your own age. During the course of the conversation, however, you begin to suspect by what the person says that he is actually much older than you because he refers to his father as though they had both grown up together. In fact, he seems to talk about his grandfather, and even his great grandfather, in the same terms. You would soon begin to think, *How could this be? This guy must be nuts!*

Such was the situation when Jesus was talking with the Jewish leaders in John 8. On several instances in that chapter, Jesus taught the people. After He had finished each lesson, the Jewish leaders came forward with questions for Him. In verse 19, they asked, "Where is thy Father?" In verse 25, they asked, "Who art thou?" When Jesus answered them truthfully, they accused Him of lying to them and of having a devil, and some even sought to kill Him.

But these confrontations all came to a head in verses 56–59. Jesus told the Jews that "Abraham rejoiced to see my day." They shot back sarcastically, "Thou art not yet fifty years old, and hast thou seen Abraham?" His response caused them to grab stones and get ready to stone Him to death: "Before Abraham was, I AM." They then knew clearly that He was claiming both His pre–existence and His deity with that statement.

All of the statements that Christ made to them were true: He had preceded Abraham because He was from the beginning; that is, He had always existed. Therefore, He must be God.

The pre–existence of Jesus and His deity are foundational truths of Christianity. We examine them in this lesson.

Student Work

He is no Christian who lives such that he does not meditate much on Christ. Some people may abound more in the work of meditation than others, some people may be more able than others, but all true Christians will meditate on Christ.

John Owen said, "If our minds are not filled with these things [i.e., meditations on Christ]—if Christ doth not dwell plentifully in our hearts by faith—if our souls are not possessed with them…we are strangers unto the life of faith!"

Why does a Christian think about Christ often? Because he loves Him. And why does he love Him? Because of the following two things:

- We love Him principally and ultimately for what He is
- We love Him immediately for what He did

Of these two reasons for loving Christ, what He did for us is that which *first* attracts us to Him. This, in turn, directs our hearts to consider what He is in Himself, and thus, our love is finally fixed on Him (or His person). This is the method of Scripture; it first proposes to us what the Lord has done for us, and then it leads us to consider His person.

Read Philippiains 2:5–11; 3:8–11.

Of what does God speak in 2:5–11, His work or His person? _____ _____ Now note Paul's response in 3:8–11. To what is he attracted and attached in this passage, His work or His person? _____

_____ Thus, we see the scriptural order. First, we are attracted to His work and fall at His feet in worship, but then we want to know personally the One who did this great work. Thus, in our study of the worth (preciousness) of Christ, we will first observe His work (His history) and then His person.

Christ's Deity

A study of the pre–existence of God answers the age–old argument concerning the deity of Christ. Those who deny the deity of Christ (i.e., that Christ is God) deny the pre–existence of Christ; for if Christ existed before His birth, then obviously He is not mere man.

Several theories are advanced in an effort to deny the pre–existence of Christ, including the following two theories.

1. He Is the Son of God; Therefore, He Had a Beginning

This argument is based on the logic that all sons descended from their fathers. Therefore, Christ, being the Son of God, must have begun *after* God the Father. If He began after God the Father, then obviously He is not God.

A study of the pre–existence of Christ, however, destroys this argument. As we note in the teacher's lesson, Christ created _____ _____ (John 1:3), and without Him was not _____ made that _____.

Read Ephesians 3:9. What do we learn there concerning Christ's work *before* He was born as a human in Bethlehem? _____ _____ .

Now read Colossians 1:15–17. What do these verses state about Christ? _____ _____ _____

Note especially v. 17. What two things does it say about Christ?

- • and_____
- • and_____

(The word *consist* means "hold together.") That is, Christ is not only the Creator but also the very power that holds everything in the universe in place! Therefore, gravity is nothing but the power of Christ!

Obviously, if Christ made *all* things, He could not have had a beginning. Without Him was not *anything* made that was made—including Himself.

2. He Was Only a Thought or an Idea in God's Mind

This argument is mentioned in the teacher's lesson. It states that "Christ" has always existed but not as a real person. Before the world existed, He was in existence but only as a *future idea* in the mind of God. One day, God took that idea back into His mind; thus, "Christ" will live forever in the memory of God.

How do we refute this argument? _____

_____

_____

_____

Christ's Eternality

Prophecy States That Christ Existed Before His Birth in Bethlehem

How is this fact seen in Micah 5:2? _____

_____

Micah claims that Christ has existed from _____

Christ Claimed His Own Pre–existence

How does John 17:5 show Jesus claiming to have existed before His birth in Bethlehem? _____

_____

_____

Read Exodus 3:14. God gave Moses instructions so that the Israelites would accept him as their human leader. Whom did God tell Moses to say had sent him? _____

The Hebrew word for "I AM" is a name for God from which we get the name *Jehovah* (God's most holy name).

Read John 8:58. What did Jesus say in this verse? _____

_____

Thus, the Jews understood clearly by Christ's use of this phrase that He was saying that *He* was the *I AM* who had spoken to Moses in the burning bush! It was this claim (i.e., pre–existence and deity) for which they sought to stone Him and eventually crucified Him.

Notes from the Teacher's Lesson

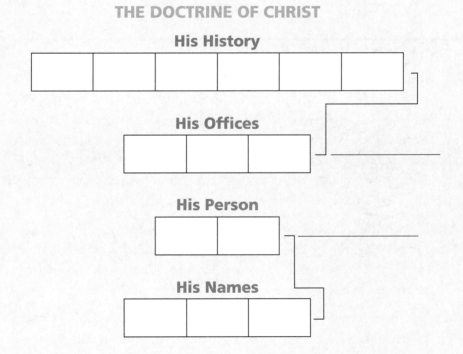

THE DOCTRINE OF CHRIST

His History

His Offices

His Person

His Names

CHRIST'S PRE–EXISTENCE

Defined: _____

_____

Stated: _____

Significance:

	Scripture	Meaning	Application
Fact	In the beginning		
Form	With God		
	Was God		
	Made by Him		
	Light of men		
Faith	Believe on His name		

Application Activities

1. Read and study John 8 in its entirety. Make a script of every statement Christ made about Himself, every question or comment that the Jews directed toward Him, and His responses to those questions or comments. What were the Jews' reactions to each of His responses? What was the reaction of the common people who heard Christ's teachings? Share your findings with the class, either in a written paper or orally in a class discussion.

2. Discuss the following questions in class. Why do you think the enemies of Christianity are so vociferous in their attacks on the doctrines of the pre–existence and Deity of Christ? What is our best defense against such attacks?

3. Discuss the following concept in class: A believer is immortal until God is finished with him or her here on earth. How should this truth be an encouragement and a comfort to every believer. Why were

Jesus' enemies unable to kill Him in spite of the fact that many of them actually took up stones to throw at Him with that very intent in mind?

4. Make an annotated list of other Scripture verses or passages that teach the pre–existence and/or deity of Jesus.

5. Make a chart or poster showing what other religions and cults teach concerning the pre–existence and deity of Jesus. List beneath each such belief verses that refute it.

6. Conduct a study of what Jehovah's Witnesses and Mormons (and other cults) say about the pre–existence and deity of Jesus. Write a Bible–based refutation of their view.

C H A P T E R   2 3

THE INCARNATION OF CHRIST

"Upon our fall from God, our nature became odious to Him…. It was so odious to God that He could not endure to look upon us. Christ taking our flesh, makes this human nature appear lovely to God."

—Thomas Watson, *A Body of Divinity*

"Oh, isn't he cute!" Kristen said as she pointed to the little baby lying in the cradle of the manger scene. "I can just imagine baby Jesus looking just like him."

"Yeah," agreed Alyson. "And he's not crying or squirming or anything. I can't picture baby Jesus ever crying or being bad for Mary and Joseph while He was…."

"Oh, look!" Kristen interrupted. "Here come the shepherds! And right behind them are the wise men!"

"Hey! Those wise men aren't supposed to be in the scene yet! They didn't visit Jesus at the manger; He and His parents were living in a house, and he was a young child by that time."

"Oh, what difference does it make, anyway, Alyson? They just add to the whole spirit of the Christmas scene. Shhhh! They're beginning to sing. Let's listen."

That's how most people react to the Christmas story today. It's just a nice little story of the birth of a baby in a lowly little manger bed with all the animals standing quietly around and the shepherds and wise men worshipping the Christ Child and offering Him gifts and the angels singing in the heavens. And that's about as much as most people know—or care—about the story.

In reality, however, it goes much deeper than that. This wasn't just *any* baby; it was God the Son taking upon Himself a body of flesh so that He could live among men, die for their sins, and then offer His death as a propitiation so they would be acceptable to God the Father. That manger scene was the site of the ultimate condescension: God became flesh. This was not just any birth; it was the incarnation.

This doctrine is a mind boggler. Even John Owen, an astute Puritan theologian, admitted, "I know in the contemplation of [Christ's glory in His condescension and incarnation] it will quickly overwhelm our reason, and bring our understanding into a loss; but unto this loss do I desire to be brought every day...."

Perhaps the simplest, most succinct definition of the doctrine was offered by Thomas Watson, who wrote, "In the creation, man was made in God's image; in the incarnation, God was made in man's image...."

As mystifying to human reason as the incarnation is the manner in which it came about—the virgin birth. This doctrine is critical to biblical Christianity.

Someone supposedly asked William Jennings Bryan, presidential candidate and defender of traditional Christianity in the early twentieth century, "Why do you emphasize the virgin birth? The Bible itself mentions it only twice." He wisely replied, "How many times does God have to tell us something before we believe it? If He mentions something only once in His Word, that is all a person needs to know it is a fact!"

The incarnation and virgin birth of Jesus Christ. These are the issues about which we'll try to gain a better understanding in this lesson.

We continue our study of Christ's history by looking at His incarnation and virgin birth. Although Christ did not begin at Bethlehem (as we learned in the previous lesson), the occurrence in that tiny village on the side of a hill three miles south of Jerusalem is very significant to human history. It will bless the heart of all who will study the birth of Christ with the same reverence that the shepherds had when they first heard the startling message of the angels.

Notes from the Teacher's Lesson

Christ's incarnation defined: _____
_____
_____

Theophany: _____
_____

Stated: _____
_____

Significance: _____

- _____

    How? _____
    _____

- _____

    How? _____
    _____

Student Work

Read Luke 1:5–13, 26–38, 46–56. Then complete the rest of the student lesson.

Divine Timing

First, we note that Christ's birth was according to a precise time in God's calendar. How is this seen in Galatians 4:4? _____

_____

_____

_____

The first promise of the birth of Christ is recorded in Genesis 3:15. Read this verse. Jesus, the Christ, is the *her seed* and the *it* of this verse. Satan is the *thee* and the *thy seed* of the passage. According to this verse, what will Christ do to Satan? _____

What will Satan do to Christ? _____

Where was this prophecy to be fulfilled? _____

_____

The "seed of the woman" is first prophesied in the Garden of Eden. For more than four thousand years, men waited for this prophecy to come true, but God was in no hurry. He had a plan, and He would not send His Son until the "fulness of time" had come. God would take four thousand years to get the world ready for the Redeemer. Note the perfection of the situation (as seen in the following points) when Christ was born.

The Roman Government Was in Power

The Roman government had built an *elaborate road system*, making it easier for the gospel to be spread faster and farther than would have been possible before they came to power.

There was *less idolatry in Israel.*. In fact, the Jewish people were tired of centuries of worshipping idols. (Perhaps they had learned this lesson during their seventy years of captivity in Babylon.) They were looking for a new form of worship.

The world was *united*. The excellent road system and the great and wide conquests of the Roman emperors had united the world and enforced a peace heretofore unknown, thereby making communication easier.

The Romans also introduced a form of capital punishment called *crucifixion*. Think of it! The world had known nothing of this form of death until its introduction by the Romans. God was waiting for this horrifying, blood–shedding method of execution, for "without shedding of blood is no remission" of sins (Heb. 9:22).

The Greek Culture Had Saturated the World

One common language was spoken throughout the world—Greek. This language was beneficial in accomplishing two goals: (a) communicating the gospel and (b) writing the New Testament. This language had a beauty of expression that was especially suited to God's purpose of expressing precisely what He meant to say to man.

The Jews Were Restless

The Jews were discontented under the rule of the Romans. They longed to be free. They were looking for a leader who would lead them to freedom as Moses had led them from Egypt. They were experiencing a revival of interest in the long–forgotten prophecies of a coming Messiah.

Thus, we see God's perfect timing. He still has a schedule today. God has a time to _____ (Heb. 9:27) and a time for _____ _____ (2 Cor. 6:2).

When your time comes, will *you* be ready? Have you trusted Christ? If not, then *today* is the day of your salvation *if* you will trust Him now as your Lord and Savior.

Divine Selection

Read Luke 1:5–13, 26–27.

God not only had a time when Christ was to be born but also He chose the very place in which and the person through whom He would be born. Nothing God does is by accident. Note how God gradually narrowed His selection of the place and person through whom Christ would come.

God's Narrowing Prophecies

- First, He will be born of the "seed of woman," or the *human race* (Gen. 3:15).

- Second, He will be born of one branch of the human race, or of _____ (Gen. 12:1–3).

- Third, He will be born of one tribe of Abraham's seed: _____(Gen. 49:10).

- Fourth, He will be born of _____ (Isa. 7:14).

- Fifth, He will be born in the village of _____ _____ (Mic. 5:2). (This prophecy was uttered 700 years before His birth!)

God's Sovereignty and Authority

Thus, we see God's absolute sovereignty and authority to plan and accomplish whatever He desires in the lives of men and the history of the world.

Divine Miracle

Read Luke 1:34–38.

How is the birth of Christ a miracle? Note the following points.

He Was Born of a Woman Who " _____ " (Luke 1:34)

That is, she was a virgin. Read Luke 1:37. How can we explain such a miracle? _____

Is a virgin birth such a miracle or hard thing for God? He created the whole universe by a simple word! He parted the Red Sea and allowed the Israelites to pass over. He halted a spinning world at Joshua's request for an entire day. He gave Abraham and Sarah a child when they were 100 and 90 years old, respectively. Is it any greater "miracle" for God to cause

Christ to be born of a virgin? The miracle is only a miracle to man. It is perfectly normal for an omnipotent God.

Why Was His Virgin Birth Necessary?

Christ had to have a human body to take our place on the cross, but He must not have our fallen human nature. He had to take upon Himself a human body, but He had to remain without sin. Thus, He came of a woman, received a human body, and was thereby made in the " _____

_____ " (Phil. 2:7) so that He could humble Himself and become "_____

_____ " (Phil. 2:8).

To deny the virgin birth is to deny salvation by Christ, for if Christ is not virgin born, then He has our fallen nature, and if He has our fallen nature, His death could not atone for our sins as only a "pure, spotless" lamb could die for man (1 Pet. 1:18–19). Thus, *the power of the cross is in the purity of His conception.*

Divine Praise

Read Luke 1:46–56. Who do we find praising the Lord in this passage? _____ What attributes of God are uppermost in her mind as she contemplates the virgin birth? _____

_____

To experience Christ is to praise Him! Anyone who has had a living experience with the Lord will have praise on his or her lips for Christ. The reverse, however, is not necessarily true. Not everyone who is shouting and praising "Jesus" has had a true salvation experience.

Someone has said that those who have no *praise* on their lips have no *person* in their heart!

Note the following three ingredients of Mary's praise to God.

Magnification (v. 46)

First, Mary magnified the Lord. *Magnify* means "to make that which is far away near." She brought Him near (enlarged Him to those around her) in two ways.

- Her spirit and soul magnified the Lord through speech and radiant, bubbling personality.
- Her body magnified the Lord through her actions and deeds.

Rejoicing (v. 47)

She rejoiced in the Lord. Do *you*? Does He literally *thrill* you? Is your spirit running over with excitement and energy because of the Lord's goodness to you? In what do you delight?

Remembrance (vv. 48–55)

She remembered the following three things. (Record the phrase that best states each.)

- She was nothing—_____
  _____

- She was somebody —_____
  _____

- He was everything—_____
  _____

How different we would be if we could keep these three things uppermost in our minds. We are nothing in ourselves; in fact, we are *less* than nothing. Yet, in Christ we become "blessed." However, may we never forget that the "somebody" we are is only because of Christ! I am still nothing. He, however, makes me somebody because He lives in me, and He is everything!

All that I have, all that I am I owe to Christ. What a Savior!

Application Activities

1. Roman Catholics place great emphasis on the virgin Mary, raising her to unbiblical and unscriptural heights (e.g., teaching that not only Jesus but also she was born without sin), whereas Bible believers place the emphasis on the virgin birth as the only acceptable means of God's becoming flesh. Refute the Catholic position and show the proper view of Mary's role in the incarnation.

2. Explain the following statement by Dr. Bob Jones, Jr.: "Essential to, and inseparable from, the incarnation is the virgin birth. For a man to say that he believes in the one and not in the other is to state an impossible thing. Indeed, the one presupposes the other."

3. Although He was born of a virgin, and therefore was without a sin nature, Jesus had a normal human development. Using Luke 2:52 as your foundation text, explain the areas in which Jesus grew and developed as any normal human being would from birth to adulthood. Also explain the various weaknesses He encountered that showed that He had the same body as everyone else.

4. Read and report on chapter 4 ("The Glory of Christ's Humbling Himself") in John Owen's book *The Glory of Christ*. (Bibliographic data are given in the Recommended Reading List.)

5. Research the account of Bridey Murphy, and summarize your findings to the class orally or in writing.

CHAPTER 24

THE IMPECCABILITY AND ATONEMENT OF CHRIST

"A great many people are trying to make peace, but that has already been done. God has not left it for us to do; all we have to do is enter into it."

—D. L. Moody, *The New Book of Christian Quotations*

In her famous hymn "To God Be the Glory," blind poet Fanny Crosby summarized the doctrine of the atonement. The second verse reads,

> O perfect redemption, the purchase of blood!
>   To every believer the promise of God;
>   The vilest offender who truly believes,
>   That moment from Jesus a pardon receives.

Many other great hymns of the faith by now–famous hymn writers teach and celebrate the role that Christ's blood plays in God's plan of salvation. Among these are "Alas! and Did My Savior Bleed?" and "At the Cross" (Isaac Watts); "Arise, My Soul, Arise" (Charles Wesley); "Hallelujah, What a Savior" and "Rock of Ages" (Augustus Toplady); "Jesus, Thy Blood and Righteousness" (Nicolaus von Zinzendorf, translated from German by John Wesley); "To God Be the Glory," "Glory to His Name," and "Are You Washed in the Blood?" (Elisha Hoffman); and "There Is a Fountain Filled With Blood" (William Cowper). And these are only a sampling of such hymns devoted to the doctrine of the atonement of Christ. Surely this doctrine is critical to the message of God to man!

We have now studied two aspects of Christ's history: (a) His _____
_____ and (b) His _____
_____ .This lesson looks at
both His sinless life on this earth and His death.

Notes from the Teacher's Lesson

His impeccability defined: _____
_____

His impeccability stated: _____

Significance of His impeccability:

- _____
- _____
- _____
- _____

His atonement defined: _____
_____

- Reconciliation— _____
  _____

- Propitiation— _____

His atonement stated: _____

Significance of His atonement:

- His blood _____

  - Holiness _____
    _____

  - Justice _____
    _____

- Love _____
_____

- Mercy _____
_____

- His blood _____.

CHANGES WROUGHT BY CHRIST'S ATONEMENT

Redeemed Man's Condition
- Alive to God
- Innocent
- Child of God
- Has a Purpose, Hope

Redeemed Man's Condition
- Dead in Sin
- Condemned
- Stranger to God
- Without Purpose, Hope

Student Work

His Impeccability

Jesus Christ was the only sinless man who ever lived on this earth. No other being with a conscience unclouded by the memory of any sins has ever lived on this earth. For example, read the following verses and write down what they say about this topic.

- Isaiah 6:5 – Isaiah explained, "_____
  _____
  _____
  _____
  _____."

- Psalm 51:3 – David cried, "_____
  _____
  _____."

- 1 Timothy 1:15 – Paul said, "_____
  _____
  _____."

- Job 40:4 – Job admitted, "_____
  _____
  _____."

Yet, Jesus Christ never expressed guilt, remorse, or contrition. He taught His disciples to pray, "Father, forgive us our debts"; yet, never once was He known to pray, "Father, forgive *Me*." On the cross He cried, "Father, forgive them."

Peter Bayne said, "No vice that has a name can be thought of in connection with Jesus Christ. Ingenious malignity looks in vain for the faintest trace of self–seeking in His motives; sensuality shrinks abashed from His celestial purity; falsehood can leave no stain on Him who is incarnate truth; injustice is forgotten beside His errorless equity; the very possibility of avarice is swallowed up in His benignity and love; the very idea of ambition is lost in His divine wisdom and divine self–abnegation."

At least four things testify to Christ's sinlessness.

1. The Witness of Scripture

- 1 John 3:5—_____
- 1 Peter 2:22— _____
  _____

- 2 Corinthians 5:21— _____
  _____

- Hebrews 4:15— _____
  _____

2. The Witness of Christ Himself

   - John 8:46—_____
     _____

   - John 14:30— _____
     _____

3. The Witness of His Friends

   - Acts 3:14 – Peter— _____
     _____

   - 1 Peter 3:22— _____
     _____
     _____

4. The Witness of His Foes

   - Matthew 27:19, 24 – Pilate and his wife—_____
     _____
     _____
     _____
     _____

   - Mark 1:24 – The demons— _____
     _____

One must remember, however, that Jesus' perfection did not consist merely in the absence of fault. Throughout His whole life, He was characterized by positive and active holiness. The more closely one analyzes His whole life, the more completely His perfection shines out.

The Atonement

In Galatians 2:20, we find the heart of the atonement: "…Son of God, who _____ me and gave _____ ."
In these three simple words—"himself for me"—is enshrined the mystery of the ages. The great intellectuals and the greatest Bible scholars of all time have all failed to plumb completely the infinite depths of the death of Christ on the cross. Paul gave his life that he might know but one thing: "Christ and him _____" (1 Cor. 2:2). Yet, after a lifetime of study and meditation on this vast subject, Paul declared, "O the _____
both of the _____ and _____
of God! How_____ are his _____
and his _____ past finding out" (Rom. 11:33).

Such a vast subject cannot be dealt with adequately in a few paragraphs, but time will not permit more than a quick glimpse into this vast truth upon which all other truths in the universe hinge. Consider, for example, the following gems of truth.

The Character of His Atonement

Read each of the following verses. Then read each of the following paragraphs, and place after each paragraph the reference that shows that characteristic of Christ's death.

Isaiah 53:6	John 10:17–18	Acts 2:23
2 Corinthians 5:21	1 Peter 2:24	1 Peter 3:18

Christ's atonement was…

Substitutionary

Substitution means "one life given for the life of another." Christ died in our place; He bore our sins; and He paid the penalty due our sins. *Substitution* as used in the Bible, then, means that something happened to Christ, and because it happened to Him, it need not happen to us. He died for our sins; therefore, we need not die for them if we accept His sacrifice. He suffered the fires of God's wrath on the cross; therefore, we need not suffer such wrath. He endured the pangs of hell on the cross; therefore, we need not endure such torment. Praise God for such a substitute! If He had not taken our place, such suffering, eternal suffering, would still await us.

Verse(s): _____

Volitional

Volitional means that Christ suffered willingly and voluntarily for our sins. He was not forced to do so. God did not have to twist His arm; Satan did not trap Him. His death was no accident. Christ willingly gave His life–blood for our salvation. Oh, the matchless grace and love of our matchless Savior!

Verse(s): _____

Predetermined

That Christ died on the cross was no accident. God the Father, Son, and Holy Spirit had planned this glorious redemption in the eternal ages long before the world was ever created. The death of Christ was the very purpose of Jesus' birth and coming to earth. God the Son strode majestically to the cross as a conqueror, although Satan thought that he led Him to the cross as a beaten captive. Little did mankind know as they drove those nails through His wrists that they were but fulfilling the most glorious plan of the ages.

Verse(s): _____

The Consequences of His Atonement

Read the following verses and place them with the proper results of the death of Christ (as you did in the preceding exercise). You may use some of the references twice.

Matthew 26:28	John 12:31–32	Romans 5:9
Romans 5:10	Romans 8:19–23	Galatians 3:13
Ephesians 1:7	Colossians 1:20	1 Timothy 2:6
Hebrews 2:14–15	Hebrews 9:15	Hebrews 10:10
Hebrews 10:19–22	1 Peter 1:18–19	2 Peter 3:13
1 John 2:2	1 John 4:10	

- **Forgiveness**

His blood paid for our sin and provided the grounds whereby a just God could forgive man. Sin must be punished. Justice will not overlook sin; it must be dealt with. Thus, God could not overlook or forgive the slightest sin in man without violating His justice. However, because Christ bore the punishment for our sins, God can be just and forgive our sins when we accept Christ's blood as payment.

Verse(s): _____

- **Removal of the Fear of Death**

Those who accept Christ as Savior and Lord need never fear death, for the sting of death has been removed. Although we may still die, to "be absent from the body" is to be "present with the Lord." As D. L. Moody said upon the day of his death, "This is my coronation day!"

Verse(s): _____

- **Redemption**

To redeem means "to purchase from the marketplace." Man is a slave to sin, "sold under sin," and is doomed to serve sin all the way to hell. However, Christ paid the price necessary to purchase sin's slaves and set us free from its curse. The purchase price was His precious blood. Had he not died, we would be hopelessly chained to sin's doom.

Verse(s): _____

- **Sanctification**

Sanctification means "to set apart for a particular purpose." When Christ redeemed us (purchased us), He did so for a purpose. He owns us and intends for us to carry out His purpose of bringing glory and honor to His name.

Verse(s): _____

- **Remission**

To remit means "to put away." Our sins have not been merely covered over but have been completely removed by the blood of Christ. They no longer exist! They are forever "blotted out," never to be remembered again. And the wonderful thing is that even our future sins are already remitted! That is why God says that nothing shall ever be able to separate us from the love of God. There is no sin in the past, present, or future that has not been forever remitted to those who trust Him.

Verse(s): _____

- **Access to God**

Access to God is through prayer. Through the blood, God has opened up direct access to heaven for the believer. We can pray directly to God without the aid of a priest. Whatever we need, insignificant as it might be and as unworthy as we are, we can go directly to the Creator of the universe and know that He hears, cares, and will answer!

Verse(s): _____

- **Reconciliation**

To reconcile means "to bring harmony or make peace between parties." When man sinned, a holy God had to turn His back on man; man, in turn, set his heart against God. He does not seek God. He does not desire God. Everything he wants is against the holiness of God. Christ came to turn man back to God, but the grounds of this reconciliation was the blood. The blood points man back to his Maker and provides the grounds whereby the Spirit can turn man's heart (by giving him repentance and quickening him) to trust Christ as Savior.

Verse(s): _____

- **Justification**

To justify means "to make innocent of sin and to declare righteous." God not only forgives our sins but also, because they are remitted (and no longer exist), can declare us righteous and accept us "in Christ" as though we had never sinned! In God's sight, we are perfect in Christ.

Verse(s): _____

- **Heirs of God**

Through Christ's blood, we are "born again" as His children. He then makes us heirs to all that is His! Thus, we have an inheritance in heaven that we cannot lose—all because of the blood of Christ!

Verse(s): _____

Its Effect on God—It Provides Propitiation

The death of Christ satisfied God's holiness and justice and opened the gate for His love, grace, and mercy to work. Until God was satisfied, grace could not save. Nothing we could do would ever satisfy a holy God. Only the shed blood of His own Son would suffice.

Verse(s): _____

Its Effect on Satan—It Overcame Him

Satan was totally defeated by the cross. What he thought was his great moment of triumph has become his utter downfall. Although he is still working to prevent everyone he can from trusting Christ, his doom is sealed. The cross sealed his coffin and chained him to the fate of the bottomless pit, into which he will be thrown to stay forever.

Verse(s): _____

Its Effect on the Universe—It Reconciled It

The whole universe was somehow cursed by God due to man's sin. Thus, it grows thorns, convulses with earthquakes, and is ravished by storms. Its animals eat and devour one another, and vegetation, animals, and planetary bodies experience degeneration and death. However, the universe will one day be renovated, "reborn," and will be made perfect because of His blood.

Verse(s): _____

Its Effect on the Law of God—It Meets Its Claims

The law of God demanded perfection with death as the penalty for anything short of absolute perfection. Thus, man was hopelessly doomed until One came who met those absolute demands with absolutely impeccable perfection. Thus, the law has no more claim on the man who accepts Christ as his substitute. The curse of the law was taken by Christ.

Verse(s): _____

Application Activities

1. Conduct a study of the Old Testament sacrifices (especially the Passover) and show the similarities between them and the sacrifice of Christ on the cross.

2. Read and report on chapter 3 ("The Sacrifice of Isaac") and chapter 10 ("The Passover Lamb") of Robert T. Ketcham's book *Old Testament Pictures of New Testament Truth*. (Bibliographic data are given in the Recommended Reading List.)

3. Except for the account of His visit to the temple at the age of twelve years, we know little about the childhood of Jesus. [Some extrabiblical writings (e.g., "The Infancy Gospel of Thomas") give some stories about it, but we have no evidence whatsoever that they are accurate. In fact, most of them are stories concocted by the Roman Catholic Church or various heretical cults.] However, using what we *do* know about the nature and character of Jesus Christ, what conclusions can you make concerning His childhood years? (Give Scripture references to support your conclusions.)

4. Make a list of other (in addition to those listed at the beginning of this chapter) famous hymns that address the doctrine of the atonement. Select one of the hymn writers mentioned at the beginning of this chapter and conduct a study of his or her life, looking especially for any things that would indicate why they emphasized the atonement in their works.

CHAPTER 25

THE RESURRECTION OF CHRIST

"Christ's rising [from the dead] is a pledge of our resurrection."

"As the first-fruits is a sure evidence that the harvest is coming, so the resurrection of Christ is a sure evidence of the rising of our bodies from the grave."

—Thomas Watson, *A Body of Divinity*

According to *Manners & Customs of the Bible* by James M. Freeman, in Roman times in Palestine, when someone died and was buried in the rock tombs in the hillside gardens, a large stone disk like a millstone was rolled in front of the opening to close the tomb. Running in front of the doorway was a deep trench, perhaps a foot or more below the doorway of the tomb. The trench, which was often along an inclined plane, held the disk-shaped stone. Once inserted into the trench, it rolled easily down the incline and across the opening, but moving it back *up* the incline to open the tomb required the greatest exertions of many strong men. That's why Mary and the other women, as they entered the garden early that morning, asked themselves who might be around to roll back the stone for them. They certainly couldn't have done it themselves.

As if the stone itself weren't enough of a problem for them, the tomb had been sealed. The stones that were placed in front of some tombs of the day were fastened at the entrance with cement. In other cases, a cord was stretched across the door-stone. A lump of stamped clay was then attached to each end of the cord. Once the clay had dried, no one could gain access to the tomb without their entrance being detected by the broken seal. Perhaps this, too, was on the minds of the women that morning.

In neither case, however, did the women have anything about which to worry. When they arrived at the tomb, the stone was already rolled away—and Jesus was gone!

Does it matter very much whether Christ rose from the dead? After all, wasn't it His *death* that provided the way of salvation? Then why argue whether He arose? The important thing is that He died, right?

Wrong!

Paul answers this question in 1 Corinthians 15:14–19. Read this passage and then list six major problems that, according to these verses, we will experience if Christ is *not* risen from the dead.

- v. 14—_____

  _____

- v. 14—_____

- v. 15—_____

  _____

- v. 17(b)—_____

- v. 18—_____

  _____

- v. 19—_____

Thus, the resurrection is the very *keystone* of the following:

- Our faith
- Preaching
- Witness
- Forgiveness of sins
- Hope and life beyond the grave
- Present joy and hope for the future

Notes from the Teacher's Lesson

Christ's Resurrection Defined

False views: _____

_____

True view: Jesus Christ arose _____ and
_____ from the grave, by the _____
_____, three days after His crucifixion, and
_____ by many
_____ to the disciples.

His Resurrection Stated

- In the Gospels—_____

  _____

- In Acts— _____

- By Paul—_____

The Nature of the Resurrection

1. _____

2. _____

We can know that His resurrection body was the same body that was laid
in the tomb by the following supporting evidence.

1. The _____ in His hands and
   feet (Ps. 22:16; Zech. 12:10; John 20:25–29)

2. The _____ in His side (John 20:25–29)

3. He was _____ by His disciples after
   the resurrection.

4. He _____ in the disciples' presence (Luke 24:41–43).

5. His body could be _____ (Matt. 28:9).

6. His body could _____ (John 20:22).

7. He possessed _____ and _____ (Luke 24:39–40).

Significance of the Resurrection

The resurrection is the historical base (or keystone) upon which all other Christian doctrines are built. If the doctrine of the resurrection stands, all of the other doctrines stand. If the resurrection falls, the other truths also fall. This is what our passage in 1 Corinthians 15:14–19 means: "And if Christ be not risen, then is our preaching vain, and your faith is also vain. Yea, and we are found false witnesses of God; because we have testified of God that he raised up Christ: whom he raised not up, if so be that the dead rise not. For if the dead rise not, then is not Christ raised: And if Christ be not raised, your faith is vain; ye are yet in your sins. Then they also which are fallen asleep in Christ are perished. If in this life only we have hope in Christ, we are of all men most miserable."

Student Work

Verifying the Resurrection

James Montgomery Boice states, "If the resurrection of Jesus Christ demonstrates the points covered [as in the teacher's lesson here]…it is obviously the best news the world has ever heard. But we ask, 'Can any news that good be believed?'"

To answer that question, consider the following seven major evidences of the bodily resurrection of Jesus Christ.

1. The Moved Stone

• According to Luke 24:2, how did the women find the stone?

  _____

  _____ .

  Experts have estimated that a stone large enough to roll in front
  of the door of the tomb would have weighed close to a ton! Such
  gravestones as have been discovered in Israel during archaeological
  digs have verified this estimate. If this were so, then who moved the
  stone?

• Note Matthew 27:62–66. What was done to the stone when it was
  rolled into place? _____ .
  Why was this done? _____

  _____

  _____ .

  Thus, would the soldiers or any of the enemies of Christ roll the stone
  away?_____ Why or why not? _____

  _____

  _____ .

• Yet, the stone *was* rolled away. To move the stone would have required
  a number of men working for quite a long time, not only pushing
  and shoving but also breaking the seal—all the while concealing their
  activity from the guards!

2. The Empty Tomb

_____ Read Matthew 28:5–6 and John 20:3–10. We might
deny that an actual resurrection took place, but we can hardly deny that
the tomb was empty! The empty tomb has been such a formidable proof
of the resurrection through the centuries that unbelievers have invented
a number of theories to explain it away. Note the following false theories
concerning the empty tomb.

The Wrong–Tomb Theory

This is the belief that the women went to the wrong tomb that Sunday morning. How would you argue against this foolish theory?

_____

_____

_____

The Swoon Theory

- This is the view that Jesus did not actually *die* on the cross, but only swooned, or fainted. They mistakenly *thought* that he was dead and buried Him alive. The cool tomb revived Him. He then got up, unwrapped the grave clothes, moved the stone, and went forth to appear as if He had resurrected.

- Refute this theory by keeping in mind (1) Christ's physical condition, (2) the weight of the stone, and (3) the presence of the guards. How many reasons can you give to obliterate this theory?

  _____

  _____

  _____

  _____

  _____

  _____

  _____

  _____

  _____

  _____

The Stolen–Body Theory

- Some skeptics theorize that someone either stole the body or moved it. Read Matthew 28:11–15. Where did this theory originate and why? _____

  _____

  _____

- To refute this theory, we simply ask the question, "Who stole the body?"

- Would some of the disciples steal it? Why or why not?

  _____

  _____

  _____

  _____

- If the enemies had stolen the body, what would they have done when the disciples began preaching the resurrection?

  _____

  _____

The Infidel's Theory

- Some people are so depraved in their thinking that they would not believe that Christ arose even if they had personally seen Him alive after His death or actually saw it happen! Ernest Renan was one such infidel. He said, "I would not believe Jesus rose, even if I saw it."

- What does Luke 16:31 teach us concerning this kind of attitude? _____

  _____

  _____

3. The Grave Clothes

- According to John 20:6–7, the tomb was not *quite* empty! What was in the tomb when the disciples arrived and looked inside?

  _____

  _____

- Every society has its distinct modes of burial. In Israel, bodies were wrapped in linen bands that enclosed nearly one hundred pounds of dry spices. The bodies were placed face up without a coffin in tombs generally cut from the rock of the Judean and Galilean hills. Many such tombs still exist in Israel. The bodies were wrapped such as to leave the face, neck, and the upper part of the shoulders bare. The upper part of the head was covered by a cloth that was twirled about like a turban.

- Thus was Jesus' body prepared for burial. The body was taken from the cross and was washed and then wrapped in linen bands. One hundred pounds of dry spices were carefully inserted into the folds of the linen. One of them, aloes, was a powdered wood like fine sawdust with an aromatic fragrance. Another, myrrh, was a fragrant gum that would be carefully mixed with powder. Jesus' body was thus encased. His head, neck, and upper shoulders were left bare. A linen cloth was wrapped about the upper part of His head. The body was then placed within the tomb.

- When the disciples arrived, they found the wrapped linen undisturbed, as though the body within had simply melted or vaporized. The linen covering for His head and face (the napkin) lay separate, as though it had simply fluttered down when His face vanished. Everything was completely undisturbed. How else can this be explained? This in itself disproves the "stolen body" theory.

4. The Frightened Soldiers

- Read Matthew 28:1–4. Describe the things that happened on the morning of the resurrection that frightened the soldiers. _____

_____

_____

_____

- This is the same information the soldiers gave to the _____ _____ (v. 11), who then _____ _____ to change their story and tell a lie. If nothing happened on that morning, if Jesus' body is still in the grave, if there is no resurrection, then why did the soldiers become so frightened? Why would they fabricate such a story. And why would the chief priests have to bribe them to change their story? Surely, something very unusual took place at that tomb that first resurrection morning.

250

5. The Bribed Soldiers

Why would anyone bribe the soldiers if there were no truth to the disciples' story? Why not just produce the body and end all of the speculation?

6. The Appearances of Christ

A careful study of Scripture reveals eleven appearances of Christ after His resurrection and before His ascension to heaven. Read the following passages and state the person(s) to whom He appeared in each instance.

- John 20:11–17— _____ , who was beside the tomb after Peter and John had left.

- Matthew 28:9–10— _____ _____, who were also returning to the tomb and saw Christ along the way. According to John Walvoord, the best texts seem to indicate that the phrase *as they went to tell His disciples* is an interpolation, and they were actually returning *after having already told* the disciples.

- Luke 24:34; 1 Corinthians 15:5—_____ in the afternoon of the resurrection day.

- Mark 16:12–13; Luke 24:13–35— _____ _____ as they walked on the road to _____. They were supernaturally blinded so that they did not recognize Him until He had explained how the Old Testament Scriptures prophesied His death and resurrection.

- Luke 24:36–43; John 20:19–23— _____ _____ as they sat at meat. Christ suddenly appeared and said, "_____" What was their initial reaction? _____ _____

    What attempts did He make to cause them to believe that He was bodily risen? _____ _____ _____

- John 20:26–29— _____

  _____

- John 21:1–23— _____

  _____

- 1 Corinthians 15:6— _____

  _____

- 1 Corinthians 15:7— _____

- Matthew 28:16–20— _____

  _____

- Luke 24:44–53; Acts 1:3–9— _____

  _____

These appearances of Christ prove beyond doubt that He arose bodily. Some people have sought to disprove the appearances by saying that they were hallucinations. How would you answer this attack logically?

_____

_____

_____

_____

_____

_____

_____

7. The Evident Change in the Disciples

- Read and compare Matthew 26:69–75 and Mark 14:66–72 with Acts 2:14–40; 5:17–42. What dramatic change is seen as a result of the resurrection of Christ? _____

  _____

  _____

- Think carefully about the following personal questions. Has your life changed? Can you honestly say that you have been transformed? What has the resurrection of Christ done for your life? Is it just a dry fact, or is it a glorious power that motivates your life and empowers you for service? How different are you as a result of having trusted in the living Christ?

- Remember, Christianity is not belief in a dead Savior or a dead creed. It is faith in a living Christ and, as such, is a religion of *life*. No one can truly trust Christ as Lord and Savior and remain the same. When one is born again, new life begins within and " _____ _____ are passed [are passing] away; behold _____ things are become [are becoming] _____" (2 Cor. 5:17).

- Has this taken place in *your* life? If not, why not trust Christ as your Lord and Savior right now? He lives to save your soul!

Application Activities

1. Research the "Shroud of Turin," which many people claim to be the authentic grave clothes of the resurrected Christ. In addition to sharing information on the shroud itself and the claims being made of it, point out some facts about the methods of burial in Palestine at the time of Christ that might tend to disprove that theory.

2. Read Matthew 28 devotionally. List all of the things you find about God in that chapter. Also record your impressions of your great God and Savior as revealed in that passage.

3. Record any providence in any category where the fact that Christ is *alive and real* was displayed or demonstrated. Even better, choose something that has happened in your life that proves beyond doubt that He is alive and is working in your life.

4. Research the origins of "Easter." Based on your findings, why might Christians prefer to refer to that day as "Resurrection Day" rather than as "Easter?" In what ways has Satan attempted to deflect attention away from the Christian significance of other major holidays (e.g., Thanksgiving and Christmas) and toward humanistic things?

5. The fact of the resurrection produced great changes in the disciples (e.g., the boldness of Peter and John). In what ways might one see changes in the lives of people today who have accepted Jesus Christ as their personal Savior? If you have accepted Christ, what changes has He produced in your life?

6. Talk to someone who has been to the Holy Land and has visited the traditional tomb of Jesus. Ask them to describe it for you. Take notes. (Or, if you have yourself been to the tomb, record your own memories of it.) Then research the location in literature (e.g., archaeology books, Bible geography books, etc.), taking careful notes. Report your findings to the class.

C H A P T E R   2 6

THE ASCENSION AND EXALTATION OF CHRIST

"In His resurrection He was exalted above the grave, in His ascension He was exalted above the starry and airy heavens, in His sitting at God's right hand He was exalted far above the highest heavens."

—Thomas Watson, *A Body of Divinity*

When a king or queen of a nation is crowned, he or she is given a crown made of the finest precious metals and rare and expensive gems (recall the British Crown Jewels mentioned in the introductory reading of lesson 21). The new monarch may also be given a scepter, representing the sovereign's temporal power. (The British Sovereign's Sceptre with Cross is a 36.5–inch–long, mostly gold rod decorated with 393 precious stones. The largest of the stones is the Cullinan I diamond, which, at just over 530 carats, is the largest top–quality cut diamond in the world.)

Some monarchs are also given an elaborately decorated and expensive orb, a symbol of the religious powers of the monarch. (The British Sovereign's Orb is 6.5 inches in diameter, weighs 42 ounces, and is decorated with more than 600 precious stones and pearls.) In the case of the British monarchy, the orb symbolizes the sovereign's headship of the Church of England.

In addition to these symbols of power, monarchs are adorned with fancy, well–tailored, and very expensive robes. Wearing these rich garments, they ascend the stairs above their subjects and sit down on an elaborate throne.

And all the people present cry out, "God save the Queen!" or "Long live the King!" or some other such acclamation to their exalted monarch.

But all of this fanfare and finery are merely temporal. Kings and queens die. They are sometimes overthrown or are forced to abdicate. At the core, when all of the crown jewels, royal clothing, symbols of power and authority, and royal prerogatives are stripped away, such monarchs are still mere men like we are.

Except for one exalted king—Jesus Christ, the King of Kings and Lord of Lords. In this lesson, we examine how He is exalted and how we who believe in Him, having bowed our knees before Him as His loyal subjects, shall one day rule and reign with Him in His kingdom.

Earlier, we studied Christ's humiliation (in His incarnation and sufferings on the cross). We now study His exaltation. In previous lessons, we saw the Sun of Righteousness in the eclipse; now we shall see Him coming out of the eclipse and shining in His full glory.

Notes from the Teacher's Lesson

His Exaltation Defined

The _____
of Christ into heaven from the Mount of _____
near _____.

His Exaltation Stated and Described

- Luke _____

- Acts _____

- Mark _____

  - It happened _____
    _____ .

- It happened _____
  _____ .

- It pictured _____
  _____ .

- It was _____
  _____ .

The Significance of the Exaltation

For Christ

- It marked both the _____
  _____ .

- It proved _____ .
- It was His _____ .
- It was His _____ .

For Believers

- His ascension _____ .
- His ascension _____ .
- His ascension _____ .
- His ascension _____
  _____ .

Student Work

The Manner of Christ's Exaltation

Christ Has Been Exalted in His Titles

God has given Jesus a name which is "_____
_____" (Phil. 2:9), that at the mere mention of His name
every "_____
_____ " and

every "_____
that Jesus Christ is _____
_____" (Phil. 2:10–11).

Thomas Watson wrote, "We must not only cast ourselves into His arms to be saved by Him, but we must also cast ourselves at His feet to serve Him."

Is He *your* Lord in actual practice? Does He literally have pre–eminence and first loyalty in your life? God has exalted His Son—have you?

Christ Has Been Exalted in His Office

As we shall study in our next lesson, Christ is our great High Priest as well as our coming King. However, He holds another office by reason of His ascension. According to Acts 5:31, what is that office? _____
_____ According to this verse, what two things does He do as our Savior? _____
_____

What an honor this is to Christ! He alone can save. Acts 4:12 says, "Neither is there salvation in _____ for there is _____ name under heaven given among men, whereby we _____ ." How it made heaven ring with the praises of the saints when Christ ascended to save our souls! One day, we will all gather before His throne and sing a new song, the words of which are found in Revelation 5:9:
"_____
_____
_____."

Christ Has Been Exalted in His Ascension

Christ's ascension was dramatic, miraculous, and triumphant.

Dramatic. Imagine the surprise and awe of the disciples as Christ dramatically raised His hands to bless them (Luke 24:50–53) and in the midst of offering His blessing His feet lifted from the ground, and He gradually began to rise as though suspended in mid–air, at first inches off the ground and then feet and yards and on up into the clouds. There has never been a more dramatic moment in history. But wasn't it fitting that the most dramatic figure that has ever walked on this earth, one who had the most spectacular birth of all creation, should leave the earth just as dramatically and as spectacularly as He had come?

What did the disciples do as He began to rise? _____

_____

_____

Miraculous. Luke 24:51 says that He was "_____" into heaven. This point indicates that a supernatural power lifted Him. Here is a true "outer–space" adventure! But Christ didn't use a rocket or a space-ship. Again, this was as it should be, for His whole life was filled with the miraculous and pointed to the supernatural. His birth was supernatural (of a virgin); His life was full of miraculous activities (turning the water to wine, feeding the five thousand, raising the dead, healing the sick, giving sight to the blind, walking on water, calming storms, etc.); His death was supernatural for He dismissed His own spirit; His resurrection was super-natural for He took His life back by His own power as a man might pick up and put on his own coat; and now He crowned His earthly ministry with His final supernatural miracle.

Triumphant. He ascended as a conqueror. He had triumphed over sin, hell, and death. His work was complete, and Satan had been utterly overthrown.

He rose to receive the spoils of His triumph. He was going back to heaven to be seated as King of Kings and Lord of Lords. The angels of heaven waited for His triumphant entry. Michael and Gabriel blew their horns at His approach. David prepared to lead heaven's choir in the "Hallelujah Chorus," and God the Father stood to greet His triumphant Son.

As glorious as this scene must have been, it was but a picture of what will one day happen to those who have trusted Him as Lord and Savior! We will experience our own ascension firsthand when He comes back for His own!

But His triumph did not stop with His arrival in heaven. He now sits exalted at the right hand of God. In the following table, note the differ-ence between His situations on earth and in heaven.

A Comparison of Christ's Situations	
Christ on Earth	Christ in Heaven
He lay in a manger.	He sits on a throne.
He was hated and scorned by men.	He is adored by angels.
His name was a reproach.	God hath given Him a name above all other names (Phil. 2:9).
He came as a servant.	He now sits as King.
He was a man of sorrows.	He is anointed with the oil of gladness.
He was crucified.	He is crowned.
His Father frowned on Him and turned His face from Him.	His Father seated Him at His right hand.
He had no form or beauty to make Him desirable to humans.	He is in the brightness of His Father's glory.

Application Activities

1. Read Philippians 2:5–11. Record all of the glorious things you see about your Savior and Lord in this passage.

2. The ascended Christ is in heaven to do three things for His children: (a) answer our prayers, (b) prepare a place for us, and (c) keep us saved. Record a providence of God in which the ascended Lord truly answered your prayer in a most unusual way.

3. If you do not already do so, begin keeping a prayer journal in which you record not only your prayer requests but also ways in which God answers those prayers.

4. Study Scripture passages that tell us how Christ acts as our Mediator and answers our prayers. Look especially for information that might affect our prayer life (e.g., when and how to pray as we ought or how to pray for the best results). Report your discoveries.

5. Read and summarize in writing chapter 5 and 6 ("The Glory of Christ's Love as Mediator" and "The Glory of Christ's Work as Mediator") and chapter 7 ("The Glory of Christ's Exaltation") in John Owen's book *The Glory of Christ*. (Bibliographic data are given in the Recommended Reading List.)

UNIT 5

THE PERSON OF CHRIST

"Christ had a twofold substance, divine and human, yet not a twofold subsistence, both natures make but one Christ...This union of the two natures in Christ was not by transmutation, the divine nature changed into the human, or the human into the divine; nor by mixture, the two natures mingled together...; but both the natures of Christ remain distinct, and yet make not two distinct persons, but one person; the human nature not God, yet one with God."

—Thomas Watson, *A Body of Divinity*

CHAPTER 27

CHRIST'S OFFICES: PROPHET, PRIEST, KING

"Ministers may set the food of the Word before you, and carve it out to you; but it is only Christ can cause you to taste it.... [Christ's priestly sacrifice] procures justification of our persons, acceptance of our service, access to God with boldness, and entrance into the holy place of heaven. Christ did not need subjects, He has legions of angels ministering to Him; but in His love He has honored you to make you His subjects."

—Thomas Watson, *A Body of Divinity*

Many jobs, especially those in small businesses, require the employee to wear a variety of hats and fulfill myriad responsibilities. For example, a small real estate business might hire an employee to a position the official job title of which is "real estate agent," meaning that his or her primary responsibility is to sell a variety of types of property. Because the business is small, however, the person who fills that position might also be expected to complete all of the paperwork involved with a sale, answer the telephone whenever he's in the office, purchase advertising for the company, and provide numerous public relations functions, such as speaking to local business or civic organizations.

Another common example of a position that requires its holder to wear many hats and fulfill a multitude of responsibilities is that of parent, both father and mother. The father, for example, is generally expected to be the primary breadwinner for the family. He works on the job, but his responsibility doesn't end there. When he comes home, he simply switches hats and begins his other jobs—taking out the trash; mowing the lawn; and maintaining the car, the appliances, and the house itself. He must function as the primary disciplinarian and the spiritual leader of the home. Beyond those responsibilities, he may also be a leader in the church, the Christian school, or civic organizations in the community. And the mother's roles are varied as well: launderer, housecleaner, childcare giver, shopper, cook, taxi driver, women's group leader, and possibly even paid worker in a job of her own.

In the Old Testament, God gave the nation of Israel prophets, priests, and kings. God anointed those individuals to their particular offices, gave them explicit directions as to how they were to discharge their duties, was present with them in the performance of those duties, and accepted their services (provided they were done according to His instructions). In the New Testament and today, however, He has united all of these offices and their various responsibilities in one person—the Lord Jesus Christ. Jesus Christ "wears many hats" and fulfills a variety of responsibilities.

This lesson takes a detailed look at what He does as our Prophet, Priest, and King.

Student Work

Christ As Our Prophet

Although when many people hear the word *prophet* they immediately think of someone who foretells the future, at its foundation the office of prophet is far more than that; a prophet is a teacher. As our prophet, Jesus Christ is the Master Teacher. Sir Edward Arnold, one of the greatest authorities on Buddhism, declared that one sentence from Christ's Sermon on the Mount is worth more than everything that Buddha ever taught. It is widely conceded that Jesus is the peerless Teacher of the ages.

Although part of a prophet's ministry is foretelling the future, it also includes two other elements:
• Receiving communication from God
• Transmitting God's communication to others

A prophet is but an instrument wholly dependent on the one who employs him. He is the voice but not the speaker, the message but not the sender, the musical instrument but not the player.

Let's look at the nature of Christ's prophetic ministry, which began after His baptism in the Jordan River.

It Was Predictive

Christ foretold numerous events. According to John 13:19 and 14:29, why did He foretell some things? _____
_____
_____

What does Christ foretell in the following references?

- Luke 21:20–28— _____
  _____

- Mark 13:2— _____
  _____

- Matthew 24 and 25— _____
  _____
  _____
  _____
  _____
  _____
  _____

It Was Authoritative

His listeners noted that Christ did not speak as their scribes did; He spoke "as one having authority." Compare the opening phrases of the prophet Isaiah in Isaiah 52:3 and the words of Christ in Matthew 23:36. How do they reveal Christ's authority? _____
_____
_____

It Was Revealing

Christ was the Revealer. John 1:18 says that He came to reveal _____
_____.

It Is Being Continued

His prophetic ministry continues today through the ministry of the Church in conjunction with the inspired Word. The Church is a prophetic institution that is to teach the truth of God. Oswald Sanders points out that "the faithful ministers of the Word today are the successors of the prophets, and continue the word of the Great Prophet who surpasses every grace and gift distributed through those who preach Him."

Christ as Priest

Through His office of High Priest, Christ fulfills our need for a mediator between a holy God and a guilty, sinful creature.

His Qualifications

Hebrews 5:1–2 clearly sets forth the necessary qualifications for a high priest: "For every high priest taken from among men is ordained for men in things pertaining to God, that he may offer both gifts and sacrifices for sins: Who can have compassion on the ignorant, and on them that are out of the way; for that he himself also is compassed with infirmity."

Fellowship with Man ("taken from among men")

According to Hebrews 2:7, how does Christ fulfill this qualification?

_____
_____
_____

Authority from God ("for men in things pertaining to God")

• The high priest could not be self–appointed. Hebrews 5:4 says, "_____
_____."

- According to Hebrews 5:5, how does Christ meet this qualification? _____

_____

_____

Morally and Spiritually Qualified

- How does Hebrews 7:25–26 describe Christ? _____

_____

_____

_____

- Is He morally and spiritually qualified? _____

His Capabilities

According to the following verses, what is Christ capable of doing as our High Priest?

- Hebrews 2:18— _____

_____

What does that mean? _____

_____

_____

_____

- Hebrews 4:15— _____

_____

- Hebrews 7:25— _____

_____

Christ is able to save completely. We have no problem for which He does not have a solution, no enemy from whom He cannot rescue us, and no sin from which He cannot deliver us.

Christ as King

Revelation 19:16 says that Christ is King of Kings and Lord of Lords. As we study history, we find that kingdoms are constantly rising and falling. Historians tell us that the world has known twenty–one great civilizations, all of which have endured only for a short time and then passed away.

Consider, for example, the following great nations of the past. Egypt was once a mighty world power, but today it is weak. It is even unable to cope with the tiny state of Israel. Babylon also was once mighty; today it is gone. (The nation of Iraq, which the Allies, led by the United States, soundly defeated in the Persian Gulf War, is only a mere shadow of the ancient Babylonian Empire.) Syria, once strong, has become a mere curiosity. The Greek and Roman empires both fell. The empire of the former Soviet Union crumbled in the late 1980s and early 1990s, and many of its former satellites have torn themselves apart with civil war and ethnic violence. And although in the wake of the collapse of the Soviet empire the United States is seemingly unchallenged and at the pinnacle of world power, even it is morally decadent and crumbling from within. Only God knows how long it can survive.

Historian Oswald Spengler believed that civilizations passed through a general cycle, similar to plants and animals and humans. Comparing this cycle with the seasons of the year, he said that nations are born and experience initial growth and prosperity (spring). Then they develop rapidly into maturity (summer). Their development begins to slow, however, as they age (autumn). And finally they enter a period of rapid decline, deterioration, and eventual death (winter). Some civilizations go through the cycle rapidly and "die" early. Others (comparatively few) avoid the mistakes of others through a study of history and enforcement of godliness and thereby "live" longer.

Following the Constitutional Convention, someone asked the venerable and wise Benjamin Franklin what kind of government they had given the people. He replied, "A republic—if you can keep it!" (As early as 60 BC, Cicero taught that *republics* tend to degenerate into *democracies*, and democracies break down into *autocracies*. Such is the process we've seen occurring in the United States in recent years.)

But long before Spengler, Franklin, and Cicero, the book of Daniel clearly described the course of kingdoms in this world. Belshazzar, King of Babylon, had given a party during the course of which he defiled the vessels from the temple of God in Jerusalem. In the midst of that party, a hand suddenly appeared and began writing on the wall of the palace. Understandably, Belshazzar was very frightened. The words read "MENE, MENE, TEKEL, UPHARSIN." No one was able to translate the foreign language. Then someone remembered Daniel, and he was brought in to translate and interpret the writing.

How did he interpret the words in Daniel 5:25–28?

- MENE— _____

  _____

- TEKEL—_____

  _____

- PERES— _____

  _____

This message describes the course of all human kingdoms. God allows a nation to rise in power, but it soon falls through the sinfulness of its people. Human powers and nations may rise and fall, but God reigns forever over all that happens in human history, even over nations and individuals who are in rebellion against Him.

What does Proverbs 21:1 say concerning this truth? _____

_____

_____

Psalm 2:2–3 says, "The kings of the earth set themselves, and the rulers take counsel together, against the Lord, and against his anointed, saying, Let us break their bands asunder, and cast away their cords from us." According to verse 4, what is the Lord's reaction to the nations that conspire against Him? _____

_____

Our puny efforts against God shall avail nothing. He is the King of kings and the Lord of lords.

Christ is our Prophet, Priest, and King. In a lesser way, we, too, are prophets, priests, and kings. We are prophets in the sense that we are to take in (i.e., receive) God's Word and then transmit it to others. What does Numbers 11:29 say concerning this point? _____

_____

_____

We are also priests. We all have direct access to the Father because of Christ's sacrifice. First Peter 2:5 reminds us that we are _____

_____

_____.

We must also exercise our priesthood by praying for each other.

Finally, there is also a sense in which we are kings with Christ. Revelation 5:10 says that he "hast made _____

_____"

How do we reign? We reign by resigning. We resign the throne of our hearts and instead put ourselves on the cross. We give Christ the throne and let Him rule our lives.

Notes from the Teacher's Lesson

CHRIST'S THREEFOLD ROLE

Christ's Offices	Prophet	Priest	King
Defined			
Stated			
Characteristics			
Significance	As Prophet–Teacher, Christ meets our need for	As Priest–Mediator, Christ meets our need for	Because Christ is King, we can

Application Activities

1. Record a providence from recent history that indicates the continuing rule of Christ over this world.

2. Read Edward Gibbon's classic work *The Decline and Fall of the Roman Empire* (bibliographic data are in the Recommended Reading List). Write a paper or give a speech summarizing the reasons for the fall of Rome. What parallels (especially spiritual and moral) do you see between Rome's national condition and that of the United States today?

3. Apply Spengler's history cycle to the nation of Israel from after the death of David until the division of the nation into two kingdoms. Then trace the cycle separately for both the northern and the southern kingdoms until their respective defeats and captivities.

4. List the aspects of the prophecy of Christ recorded in Matthew 24 and 25 that are relevant to the world situation today.

5. By studying the book of Hebrews, explain the ways in which Christ's priesthood is far better than the priesthood of the Old Testament.

6. Read Percy B. Shelley's poem "Ozymandias." Explain the message of this poem and the lesson it holds for both the believer and the unbeliever. (Optional: memorize this poem.)

CHAPTER 28

CHRIST'S DEITY

"Beware of men who speak of the divinity of Jesus.... The correct phrase is 'the deity of Christ.' There is a difference. He is not just divine: 'He is the very God of very God, One with God, coeternal with the Father."

—Dr. Bob Jones, Jr., *Fundamentals of Faith*

One A. Naismith included the following "meaty" selection in the book *2400 Scripture Outlines, Anecdotes, Notes, and Quotes*. It is a fitting introduction to the topic we are about to study in this lesson.

What do we need in God that we do not find in Christ? God is not beyond Him, but in Him. He brings God: in Him God comes—Immanuel. In Jesus Christ we meet God. He is One with the inmost heart of God. His life is a personal disclosure of the Life of God.

> *Like men He walked, like God He talked;*
> *His words were oracles, His deeds were miracles;*
> *Of God the true expression, of man the finest specimen;*
> *Full–orbed humanity, crowned with Deity;*
> *No trace of infirmity, no taint of iniquity;*
> *Behold the Man! Behold thy God!*
> *Veiled in flesh the Godhead see,*
> *Hail, Incarnate Deity!*

Having studied the history and offices of Jesus Christ, we come now to a contemplation of His person. The knowledge that a Christian has of Christ's person is more valuable than any other kind of knowledge. In Philippians 3:8, Paul, who knew how to value it, called it "the _____ Christ Jesus the Lord." He also stated that he was willing to sacrifice the loss of " _____ " and did count them but " _____ " that he might have this knowledge! This shows how precious Christ was to Paul.

But who is this One of whom we speak? The Bible does not claim that He is a great man or even a good man. Instead, it asserts that He is God manifest in the flesh. The word *deity* means "God," and when it is applied to the person of Christ it means that He *is* God. It is this aspect of His person that we study in this lesson.

Notes from the Teacher's Lesson

Christ's Deity Defined

Jesus Christ of Nazareth is _____–the _____ Person of the _____ and both the _____ and the _____ of the Old Testament.

Christ's Deity Stated

- He is God— _____

- He is the Second Person— _____

- He is Jehovah— _____

- He is the Angel of Jehovah— _____

As the Angel of Jehovah, He is…

- _____

- _____

- _____ .

    - Only the Second Person is _____ .

    - He no longer _____ .

    - Both are _____ by God.

    - By process of elimination.

The Significance of Christ's Deity

Negatively—If Christ Is Not God…

- _____
  _____

- _____
  _____

- _____
  _____

- _____

Positively—Because Christ Is God…

- _____
  _____

- _____
  _____

- _____

Student Work

Denials of Christ's Deity

Because the deity of Christ is the crucial doctrine of the Word, it has been the focal point of satanic attacks since the time of Christ's earthly ministry. Following is a brief sketch of the history of some of those who have opposed the deity of Christ.

The *Jews* wanted to stone Jesus when He taught that He was God (see earlier lessons that cover this conflict with the Jews).

The *Ebionites* and other sects first started denying the deity of Christ shortly after the first century.

Arius, who lived in the fourth century, led the most vicious attack on Christ's deity. Not until his time had anyone paid much attention to arguments against Christ's deity. The followers of Arius were called Arians.

Socinus kept the heresy alive during the Reformation. His followers were called Socinians.

In the nineteenth century, the German theologians *Ritschl* and *Schleiermacher* continued to perpetuate the false doctrine. They were the forerunners of today's liberals.

Today, more and more focus is being placed on this doctrine in an attempt to discredit it. Oswald Sanders said, "Without question, the last battle of the Christian age, as the first, will center in the Person of Christ. It is significant that most of the modern religious cults are in error concerning the Person and deity of Christ." For example, *Spiritism* asserts that "it is an absurd idea that Jesus was more divine than any other man." *Christian Science* claims, "Jesus is not God, as Jesus Himself declared, but the Son of God." And the *Jehovah's Witnesses* boldly state, "Jesus was not God the Son."

Liberals today offer the following three answers to the question of who Jesus Christ was (is).

He was a great teacher, a great man.

One group of liberals claims that He is perhaps the greatest teacher and the greatest man who ever lived, but He was nothing more. They believe that He should be followed but not worshipped. It is easy to answer this proposition: If He is not what he claimed to be, is He truly great? He would be a liar, and who could call a liar a great teacher?

He was a good man.

Other liberals consider Him a wonderful man. They preach about His sincerity, His character qualities, His courage, and His willingness to die. This is as far as they go, however. They refuse to accept the miracles as supernatural.

He was an example or a model to be followed or imitated.

Some people say that Christ "was ahead of his time in the evolutionary process" but nevertheless was still but a man.

Proof of Christ's Deity

We can offer at least five major proofs of Christ's deity.

The Scriptures Claim That He Is God

Read the following verses. State how each asserts the fact that Christ is God.

- John 1:1—_____
- John 20:28— _____
- Romans 9:5— _____
- Philippians 2:6— _____

  _____

- Titus 2:13— _____
- 1 John 5:20— _____

  _____

Divine Names Are Applied to Him

Read the following verses and list the divine names that are ascribed to Christ in them.

- Isaiah 9:6—_____
  _____

- Isaiah 40:3—_____

- Jeremiah 23:5–6—_____
  _____

- Hebrews 1:8—_____

Divine Attributes Are Ascribed to Him

A study of the life of Christ reveals attributes in Him that God alone possesses, such as the following. Read each of the following sets of verses and list the attribute of God that is evident in each.

- Isaiah 9:6; John 1:1–2; Revelation 1:8— _____

- Matthew 18:20; 28:20; John 3:13—_____

- What is unusual about the statement in John 3:13?
  _____
  _____

- John 2:24–25; Revelation 2:23—_____

- Isaiah 9:6; Philippians 3:21; Revelation 1:8— _____

- Hebrews 13:8— _____

He Performed Divine Works

Jesus Christ proved His deity by doing things that only God could do. Read the following verses. Match the references with the things that Christ did that were divine.

	John 1:3, 10	A. Forgives sin
	John 11:43–44	B. Creates
	Mark 2:7–10	C. Raises the dead
	Ephesians 1:22	D. Judges mankind
	John 17:2	E. Gives eternal life
	2 Timothy 4:1	F. Rules over the Church

Divine Honor Was Paid to Him

Another proof of His deity is the fact that He was given honor that is due only to God. How was the honor given to Christ in each of the following verses proof that He must be God?

- Matthew 28:19— _____
  _____
- John 5:23— _____
  _____
- John 14:1— _____
- Hebrews 1:6— _____

Application Activities

1. Read Hebrews 1. List all of the things you see in that passage concerning the deity and person of Jesus Christ.

2. Record a providence in your life that has helped to confirm that the salvation you have in Christ is real (i.e., how it helped prove to you that you were saved and, thus, that Christ must be who He said He is because His salvation works).

3. Conduct a research study of the beliefs of one or more of the following groups or individuals. Summarize and refute their positions on the deity of Christ.

   Arius (the Arians), Ebionites, Socinus, Ritschl and Schliermacher, Spiritism, Christian Science, Jehovah's Witnesses

4. Why do you think Satan is so intent on attacking the doctrine of Christ's deity more than any other single doctrine of the Bible? What does that say about our need to believe and study it today?

CHAPTER 29

CHRIST'S HUMANITY

"He became what we are that He might make us what He is."

—Athanasius, *The New Book of Christian Quotations*

Whenever a doctrine is stated, Satan must attack it in some way. He cannot stand to let a doctrine remain unchallenged. If he cannot destroy the doctrine itself (which he can never really do), he will try to corrupt or counterfeit it. Just as we saw this strategy used against the doctrine of His deity (and other doctrines), we also see it used to oppose the doctrine of Christ's humanity. One example will be sufficient to illustrate this fact.

Before the first century was over, people began to speculate about aspects of Christ's life that are not discussed in Scripture, especially His childhood years. Speculative stories of what He *might* have done as a child traveled widely and were soon being repeated as though He had *actually done* them. Some of these stories were printed and further circulated, including a book titled *The Infancy Gospel of Thomas*. One commentator sympathetic to the contents of that book described it thus: "The narrative begins with Jesus as a five-year-old boy and relates a number of incidents…that betray a streak of the mischievous in Joseph and Mary's precocious son. Here are anecdotes of Jesus at play with his childhood companions (sometimes harming them with his divine power, sometimes healing them), in confrontation with his elders (usually bettering them), at school with his teachers (revealing their ignorance), and in the workshop with his father (miraculously correcting his mistakes)."

Not only are these statements mere suppositions without any historical evidence but also they are in direct contradiction to what the Scriptures do tell us about Christ, His youth, and His nature (see especially Luke 2:51–52). Based on that passage alone, could you imagine Jesus Christ as "mischievous," or "harming" his playmates, or "in confrontation with his elders," or gleefully "showing up" his teachers' ignorance?

One passage from this extrabiblical account states, "The son of Annas the scribe was standing there with Joseph. He took a branch of a willow and scattered the water which Jesus had arranged. Jesus saw what he did and became angry and said to him, 'You unrighteous, impious ignoramus, what did the pools and the water do to harm you? Behold, you shall also wither as a tree, and you shall not bear leaves nor roots nor fruit.' And immediately that child was all withered."

Another passage states, "…[H]e was going through the village, and a child who was running banged into his shoulder. Jesus was angered and said to him, 'You shall go no further on your way.' And immediately the child fell down dead."

Can you imagine a *sinless* Christ doing such things or speaking such derogatory words to mere children? (Although Christ did use some strong and blunt language during His adult ministry, He was responding to the actions of *adults* who were old enough and educated enough in the things of God to know that what they were doing was contrary to God's law. He was reacting to a violation of God's law, not to a personal affront.)

Yet, many people will believe such stories. Don't be caught up with such ploys of Satan to denigrate the doctrines of God's Word. Rather, "search the Scriptures," know what they say (and don't say), and accept from men's ideas only what can be clearly supported and authenticated by the Word. To accept what cannot be supported by the Word is to open yourself to the deception of Satan. If God said it, that should settle it; if God *didn't* say it, we should suspect it.

If any fact stands out clearly in the New Testament, it is the complete and genuine humanity of Jesus Christ. Alongside the glorious truth of the deity of Christ, the Bible asserts the humanity of Christ. To hold to one of these doctrines without the other is to be in gross error on the central doctrine in all of Scripture.

The teacher's lesson points out the following four basic truths, or pillars, that must be equally understood if one is to have a proper understanding and definition of the identity of Christ:

1. Jesus Christ is _____ .

2. Jesus Christ is _____ .

3. His humanity and His deity are _____
_____ .

4. His humanity and His deity are _____
_____ .

For one to be confused on *any* of these four foundational points is to invite error.

Student Work

Evidences of Christ's Humanity

Unlike His Godhead, Jesus is not man from eternity past. He became man at a particular point in time through His incarnation (see lesson 23). Now, having become man, He is the God–man to whom alone we look for salvation.

Scripture abounds with evidence of His humanity. Note the following four evidences of this humanity.

He Had Human Parents and a Human Ancestry

We find two genealogies of Christ in the New Testament, one in Matthew 1:1–18 and the other in Luke 3:23–38. Matthew traced the *paternal* line of Christ through the kingly line of David to His mother's husband, Joseph. Although Christ did not have an earthly biological father, He was in the line of Joseph, who was married to His earthly mother. Being a descendant of the kings of Israel meant that Jesus Christ was of the house of David, as the Old Testament had predicted.

Luke, however, traced Christ's *maternal* genealogy through Mary back to the first man, Adam. Therefore, He has earthly descendants like the rest of us, with one major exception—*He had no earthly father*. Therefore, through Mary He received our nature but in a sinless state.

Another important feature of this genealogy is the number of notorious sinners it mentions in Christ's ancestral line. In these genealogies, find a descendant who…

- was a deceiver— _____

- allowed his own brother to be sold into slavery— _____

- was a wicked king (you could list several of these!)— _____
_____

- was once a harlot— _____

- committed adultery with a famous king—_____

- was a Gentile woman (from Moab)— _____

The significance of Christ's genealogy is that it links Him to and identifies Him with sinners. Because He came to die for sinners, He must be identified with us.

He Had a Human Appearance

How do you see this fact in the following passages?

- John 4:9— _____
_____

- Luke 24:13–15— _____
_____

- John 20:15— _____
_____

Jesus Christ did not look like a superman. He did not walk around with a halo over His head or an aura, or glow, surrounding Him. In fact, what does Isaiah 53:2 tell us about His outward appearance?

_____

_____

_____

He Was Subject to Sinless Human Infirmities

Like every other man, Christ suffered the same problems and human limitations with one major exception—He had no sin.

Beside each of the following references, list the things in the verse or passage that show that He suffered the same physical limitations as other men.

- Matthew 4:2— _____
- John 19:28— _____
- John 4:6— _____
- Mark 4:38— _____
- Hebrews 2:9–10; 12:2—_____

  _____
- John 11:35— _____
- Matthew 26:36–40—_____

Oswald Sanders, in his book *The Incomparable Christ*, had the following to say concerning the subject of Christ's human limitations.

Our Lord's consenting to be subject to human limitations was part of the mystery of His great self–humiliation. While in His incarnate state He did not renounce His divine powers, (still) His intelligence was so subject to human limitations that He submitted to the ordinary laws of human development. He was no exception…. He acquired His knowledge through the ordinary channels open to the other boys of His day (i.e., through instruction, study, and reflection). It would appear that He even voluntarily renounced knowledge of certain future events. According to Mark 13:32, what did He not allow Himself to know while on earth? __

Like ourselves, Jesus was *not self–sustained* but needed prayer and communion with His Father for the support of His spiritual life. In all the great crises of His life, He resorted not to the counsel of men but to prayer to His Father for guidance.

That we are in the presence of mystery here is conceded. We find it difficult to reconcile these human limitations with His possession of divine attributes. But could He not have possessed them and yet not exercised them?

One of the strongest evidences of the reality of His humanity was His experience of *human suffering*. He knew the salty taste of pain. Every nerve of His body was racked with anguish. Though He was God's Son, He was not exempt from suffering. His sufferings of body and of spirit have formed the theme of a thousand volumes. The fact that He was sinless made Him more sensitive to pain than His sinful contemporaries. We read of His "being in agony." The accompaniments of the death of the cross assure us of His ability to sympathize with human suffering.

He Had Human Names

Jesus called Himself the _____ thirty times in Matthew, fourteen times in Mark, twenty–five times in Luke, and eleven times in John—_____ times in all (John 1:51). In fact, even when acquiescing in the title "Son of God," He sometimes immediately afterward substituted the title "_____" as though to emphasize His possession of two natures in the unity of His person. Thereby He claimed to be the representative of all humanity. (We will study this aspect of Christ in more detail in the next lesson.)

Notes from the Teacher's Lesson

CHRIST'S HUMANITY

His humanity defined:

	Jesus Christ is…	Error
Deity		
Humanity		
Unity		
Distinction		

His humanity stated: _____

THE SIGNIFICANCE OF CHRIST'S HUMANITY

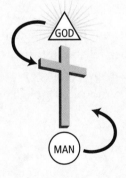

1. It qualified Him as our _____

Why did He have to be Man to die for us?

• Because He must be of _____

• Because _____ was _____

2. _____ **over** _____

3. _____

Application Activities

1. Focus on Christ in the Word. Read Isaiah 53, and record your impressions of what Christ must have gone through on this earth as man.

2. Focus on Christ in providences. Record a providence about the way in which you have experienced the fact that Christ understands what you are going through and gave you precisely the grace, mercy, strength, and/or peace you needed for that particular moment.

3. Read and study Luke 2:51–52. Explain what these verses tell us concerning the humanity of Christ. What applications does Christ's example in these verses hold forth for you personally?

4. Explain why we cannot put stock in the widely circulated nonbiblical stories of Christ's early growth and development during His childhood. In assessing such accounts, what scriptural truths must be our standards for evaluation?

5. Explain why it was necessary for Christ to have a human body. Why does the Bible put so much information on "the begats" and genealogies of its characters? What does that emphasis teach us?

6. Create your own genealogy. Begin with your mother and father, and trace each branch of your "family tree" as far back as you can. (Get your information from your parents, grandparents, aunts and uncles, etc. When you hit a snag and can obtain no further reliable information from these sources, check your local historical society or genealogical society.) Do you have any famous (or infamous!) people in your family tree? If so, tell about them.

CHAPTER 30

CHRIST'S NAMES

"Other names are dear, but [Jesus' name] is dearer."
—Herbert Lockyer, *All the Men of the Bible*

"What's in a name?" William Shakespeare asked in his famous play *Romeo and Juliet*.

Actually, there's a *lot* in a name. Just notice the lengths to which people (and businesses) will go to protect a good name or to cover a bad name. One parent regularly reminded his children whenever they left the confines of the family to attend a ball game, go to a party, or shop in the mall, "Remember who you are!" This should be especially true for one who claims to be a *Christian*.

One of the popular trends of the late 1990s was for people to wear bracelets with the letters *WWJD* engraved on them. One could also see bumper stickers, key chains, T–shirts, and other merchandise bearing the same initials. They weren't advertising for the local radio station. They were asking the readers a very important question: *What would Jesus do?*

The wearers and bearers of that slogan, however, must realize that their behavior can actually negate its message if that behavior doesn't match what Jesus would do. It's true that "actions speak louder than words"—or bracelets and bumper stickers.

If you were driving along on the highway and were suddenly, rudely, and dangerously cut off by a car bearing a WWJD bumper sticker, what would be your immediate assessment of the driver? If you heard someone who was wearing a WWJD bracelet or T–shirt curse and swear or saw them in a place where Christians shouldn't be, what would be your immediate assessment of that person? Such things happen far too often, and unbelievers notice it!

What's in a name? Plenty! A name can be very powerful—either for good or for bad. Remember who you are if you claim the name *Christian*, and act, talk, and think in such a way as to bring honor to your "family name"—Christian.

Similarly, the various names of Christ are packed with meaning and power. That is the topic to which we now turn our attention. This lesson concludes our consideration of the glorious Second Person of the Godhead. We have viewed His glorious history and His majestic person and nature. Now we focus our attention on His precious names.

Scholars have cataloged more than 150 different names for Christ that are used in the Bible. (Don't worry—this lesson will deal with only a few of those 150 names!) By studying only these few, however, you can see that to plumb the depths of the glories of our Lord is truly a life–long process. Study as much as one might, he will have only scratched the surface!

Solomon spoke of God's name as "ointment poured forth" (Song of Sol. 1:3) because His names best describe the fragrance and the glories of His person and character. Enter this lesson prayerfully, asking God to fill your heart to overflowing as you bring your finite mind into concentrated meditation on the names of the most holy and most glorious Being, the most precious Person in the universe.

Notes from the Teacher's Lesson

Christ's Names

Name: _____

    Defined: _____

_____

_____

    Stated: _____

_____

_____

    Significance:

        1. _____

        2. _____

        3. _____

Name: _____

    Defined: _____

_____

    Stated: _____

    Significance: _____

Name: _____

    Defined: _____

_____

_____

    Stated: _____

_____

Significance:

1. _____

2. _____

3. _____

Student Work

The teacher's lesson discusses the following names of Christ. Pay particular attention to what the teacher says concerning each of them, including the definition, the Bible reference in which it is found, and its significance to you as a believer.

- Jesus
- Christ
- Lord of Glory

Other Names of Christ

This lesson discusses some other names of Christ that are not covered in the teacher's lesson.

Old Testament Titles and Names

Look up the following passages of Scripture and record the name or title of Christ that you find in each passage.

- Genesis 3:15—_____

- Numbers 24:17—_____

  _____

- Deuteronomy 18:15—_____

- Isaiah 9:6—_____

  _____

- Isaiah 7:14—_____

- Zechariah 6:12— _____

- Job 19:25—_____

- Song of Solomon 2:1—_____

  _____

New Testament Titles and Names

Of the scores of names and titles of Christ found in the New Testament, let's examine the following single name and observe but a few of the golden nuggets in it.

The Name: _____ (John 8:58, the last two words).

Read Exodus 3:14. What name did God use for Himself? _____
This name indicates *eternal present tense*. There was never a time when God wasn't. There will never be a time when Christ will not be. Therefore, the name indicates one who:
- Never began
- Will never end
- Is totally self–sufficient (i.e., needs nothing or no one to keep Himself alive, neither food, air, rest, or shelter)
- Is complete (i.e., nothing can be added to Him; therefore, if you have Him you have *everything*!)

Christ as the Great I AM

When Christ claimed this title, He was claiming deity. He was claiming to be the same person who spoke to Moses out of the burning bush! Therefore, the preceding four facts must be true of Christ if He is, indeed, the I AM. Let's look at each of them.

- He never began.

  Think back to our earlier studies of Christ. Where (both lesson number and Bible reference) do we see that Christ has always existed?_____

  _____

  _____

- He will never end.

Circle the reference that best teaches that Christ is eternal: Ephesians 3:19, Hebrews 13:8, or 1 John 3:1?

Through Christ we have an eternal…

- _____ (Eph. 3:11)

- _____ (Eph. 3:21)

It would be strange if God's purpose and glory through Christ were eternal and yet Christ wasn't!

- He is totally self–sufficient.

Jesus Christ needs nothing that He cannot supply of Himself. While He was on earth, when He and His disciples needed a coin for taxes, what did He do? (Matt. 17:24–27)

_____

_____

When He needed to feed five thousand people, what did He do? _____

_____.

When He needed wine to serve the wedding guests, what did He do? _____

When He needed to cross the lake and didn't have a boat, what did He do? _____

Truly, such a man never lived who would compare with our Christ! If He was in the midst of a storm, He could stop it immediately by only speaking to it. He could stop a funeral and raise the dead. He could speak to a tree and dry up its leaves. He could fill a net with so many fish that the net couldn't hold them all. Yes, He could lay down His own life and then take it back (John 10:18).

- He is complete in Himself.

Therefore, if we have Christ, we have all we ever need! Read the following verses, and write down the things that Christ said He was (and which all who have Him in their hearts possess).

- John 6:48, 51— _____
- John 8:12—_____
- John 10:7, 9—_____
- John 10:11— _____
- John 11:25— _____
- John 14:6—_____
- John 15:1—_____

Note especially John 15:6. As He is self–sufficient, we are completely deficient. Without Him, we are like a dead stick lying on the ground. Only as we " _____ " (v. 4) do we bear fruit.

How do we abide in Him? By fellowship with Him through meditation every day. Through Him, we can have *all that He is—and He is everything*! Whether grace, mercy, strength, power, victory, peace, consolation, or material goods, He has *all of everything* we need. Then why should we *ever* turn to the world?

Application Activities

1. Focus on Christ in the Word by reading John 17. Record all of the things that Jesus Christ has done and will continue to do for those who are saved. What do you learn about Christ in this passage?

2. Focus on Christ in providences. Record a providence in the life of a contemporary in which Christ provided just what the person needed during a time of crisis or trial.

3. Record a providence in your own life in which Christ supplied exactly what you needed at the time of need.

4. Make a list of names for Christ that are *not* covered by either the teacher's lesson or the student textbook. Give the reference for each name cited. Then check a source that will give the meaning of each name (e.g., books in Herbert Lockyer's series such as *All the Men of the Bible* and *All the Women of the Bible*). See how many of the more than 150 such names you can list.

5. What is the origin of your surname? What is the origin and meaning of your given name? Are there any lessons or applications you can make of the knowledge you gain about your names? Do you claim the name of *Christian*? If so, reread the introduction of this lesson, and take any actions necessary for you to be worthy of the name.

6. Read pp. 363–369 of Lockyer's book *All the Men of the Bible*. Write a summary of the names of Christ as discussed by Lockyer.

UNIT 6

THE HOLY SPIRIT

"The Third Person in the Trinity is the Holy Ghost, who proceeds from the Father and the Son, whose work is to illuminate the mind, and enkindle sacred emotions."

—Thomas Watson, *A Body of Divinity*

CHAPTER 31

WHO THE HOLY SPIRIT IS

"The Holy Spirit is a living Person and should be treated as a person. We must never think of Him as a blind energy nor as an impersonal force."

—A. W. Tozer, "The Divine Conquest," *A Treasury of A. W. Tozer*

Cody was troubled, and Gwen, his friend, could tell it as soon as she saw him sitting on the steps outside the school.

"Hey, Cody. What's bothering you? You look as though you're troubled."

Cody nodded dejectedly as Gwen sat down beside him on the steps. "Yeah! You could say I'm 'troubled' a little."

"Well, what is it?" Gwen pressed. "Maybe I can help."

Cody sighed deeply and then answered, "I'm a senior, right?"

"Yeah, but what's that got to do with your troubles. You should be happy about that!"

"Well, yeah, I am. But it just that the year's almost over and I still don't know what I'm going to be doing after graduation. I really *want* to do what the Lord wants for me, but…." His voice trailed off as he kicked absently at his books on the step in front of him. Then he quietly finished his thought. "I just don't know what God wants me to do."

"Oh," Gwen whispered, her voice matching Cody's. "Well, you might not know, but God does. And *He* wants *you* to know, too! I tell you what. Mr. Mathis is still in his room—I just passed by there, and he was rearranging the desks in his room. Maybe he can give you some advice. Come on. I'll go with you."

Together, they walked into Mr. Mathis's classroom. He greeted them as he shoved the last desk into the row at the back of the room.

"Well, I don't remember giving you two detention. You must have a question, right?"

Cody began to explain to Mr. Mathis the struggle he was having. "How can I know what God wants me to do?" he asked when he had finished.

Mr. Mathis shared the following information with him as Gwen sat quietly and nodded her agreement.

God reveals His will in one or more of the following ways:

- Through His Word

- Through the control of one's thought life

- Through various circumstances of life (providences)

- Through the advice of godly men or women

But before one can comprehend or even perceive His speaking to him or her through those means, he or she must meet certain prerequisites, including the following.

- *Good physical condition*. One's physical state often affects his mental or spiritual state.

- *Emotional maturity*. The more mature one is emotionally, the more clearly he will discern God's will.

- *Spiritual maturity*. The person who has grown in the Lord and is feeding regularly on "the meat of the Word" will be better able to discern the Lord's will than a person who is not growing and is content to stay on "the milk of the Word."

- *Spirit of yieldedness to God.* The person whose life is a daily "living sacrifice" (see Rom. 12:1–2) will more readily know the will of God than someone whose life is not fully yielded to obeying whatever God says.

- *Sincere desire to know—and do—God's will.* A lot of people want to *know* God's will; fewer are willing to *obey* it once they know it.

- *Daily obedience to what they do know.* God will not reveal any more of His will than you are already obeying. How can you hope to obey His will for five years from now if you aren't obeying what He has commanded you to do right now?

Cody listened intently to Mr. Mathis' words. What he was saying seemed so simple. Why hadn't *he* thought of these things before?

"But these are only a summary of what you might find in a book I have, Cody," Mr. Matthis said as he walked to a bookcase at the rear of the classroom. He looked over the books for a few moments and then selected one. "Here's a book that will help you understand the points I've mentioned," he said as he handed the volume to Cody. "Keep it as long as you like," he said with a wave of his hand. Then he added, pointing his index finger at Cody with a smile, "Just remember that it's God's will for you to return borrowed books to their owners!"

Cody thanked Mr. Mathis and walked outside with Gwen.

"What do you think?" Gwen asked impatiently.

"I'm glad I talked to you and Mr. Mathis," Cody said with a smile.

Revealing God's will is just one of many tasks that the Holy Spirit performs. The next four lessons address this and other aspects of the third person of the Godhead—the Holy Spirit. Undoubtedly, the Holy Spirit is the most misunderstood person of the Trinity, as you will learn during the teacher's lesson.

Notes from the Teacher's Lesson

The Holy Spirit

The Doctrine Defined

- The Holy Spirit is the _____ of the Godhead and is _____ with the _____ and the _____ in _____ though _____ as a _____.

The Doctrine Stated

1. He is a person _____
   - Another _____
   - Paraclete _____

2. He is God
   - _____
   - _____

3. He is Distinct _____

The Significance of the Holy Spirit

1. His Person— _____
   - He grieves _____

Speech	Attitudes
_____	_____
_____	_____
_____	_____
_____	_____
_____	_____
_____	

   - He can be insulted _____

2. His Deity—When we complain about circumstances, we complain against God.

He is the God of all circumstances.

Student Work

Further Evidences

We now consider further proof of both the person and the deity of the Holy Spirit. Actually, the Scriptures give hundreds of evidences of the personality and the deity of the Holy Spirit. Among the most obvious such evidences are the following.

His Person

Personal Pronouns Are Used of the Holy Spirit

• Read John 16:7–15. How many times is the Holy Spirit referred to as a person (by use of personal pronouns such as *He* and *Himself*)? _____ The word *he* is the Greek masculine pronoun *ekeinos* and is the same word that is used to refer to any real person.

• The remarkable thing about the use of the personal pronoun is the fact that the Greek word for *spirit* is (as you learned in the teacher's lesson) neuter and thus should have the neuter pronoun.

He Has the Characteristics of a Person

Match each of the following verses with the appropriate characteristic.

Eph. 4:30		A. He speaks
John 14:26		B. He has knowledge and intelligence
1 Cor. 2:10–12; Rom. 8:27		C. He has feelings and may be mistreated
Rom. 8:14		D. He loves
Rev. 2:7		E. He teaches
Rom. 15:30		F. He has a will
1 Cor. 12:11		G. He guides

He Works Personally with Full–Time Christian Workers

- Read the following three verses and state what part they reveal the Holy Spirit plays in the personal ministry of full–time Christian workers.

  - Acts 13:2— _____

    _____

  - Acts 16:6–7— _____

    _____

  - Acts 20:28—_____

    _____

- Hereby we see the importance of being constantly awake to the voice of the Holy Spirit. There is no other way to know God's will than by the leading of the Holy Spirit. Our ministry is actually *His* ministry; we are merely the tools He uses in His ministry. He chooses us for service, chooses where we should and should not work, and then actually places us where He wants us.

- Are you willing for Him to have you? Are you in touch with Him? If He were to call you today, would you hear Him?

His Deity

We see the deity of the Holy Spirit in the following points.

He Is Called God

The teacher's lesson noted two instances in which the Old Testament referred to *the Lord*, and the New Testament, in referring to the same passage, interchanged the name *Holy Spirit*. Other references refer to Him as *God*. For example, how is the Holy Spirit referred to as God in Acts 5:3–4? _____

_____

_____

He Is Associated with Both God the Father and God the Son

A number of times the phrase *Father, Son, and Holy Spirit* is used in the Bible. This fact alone should show us that the Holy Spirit is considered equal with yet distinct from God. One such example is in the baptismal formula found in Matthew 28:19. According to this verse, how are people to be baptized? _____

_____

Note that *name* is singular, indicating that the three persons are actually one!

He Has the Attributes of Both God the Father and God the Son

Match each of the following attributes with the correct verse.

	Psalm 139:7–10	A. Omnipotent
	1 Corinthians 2:10–11	B. Omniscient
	1 John 5:6	C. Omnipresent
	Luke 11:13	D. Eternal
	Genesis 1:2; Luke 1:35	E. Truth
	Hebrews 9:14	F. Holy
	Romans 15:30	G. Loving

Application Activities

1. Record a providence in which you felt a definite impression that the Holy Spirit was doing something and you obeyed His leading. How did He use you in that circumstance?

2. Using *Nave's Topical Bible* (or a similar reference), read every verse that deals with the *person* of the Holy Spirit. List everything those verses tell about the identity of the Holy Spirit.

3. Read and outline chapters 1–5 of Book III ("What the Bible Teaches About the Holy Spirit") of *What the Bible Teaches* by R. A. Torrey. (Bibliographic data are given in the Recommended Reading List.)

4. What is God's will for *you*? Make a list of things that you know are God's will for you personally. (Some of those things will also be true for every believer, but many of them should be things that are unique to you as an individual.)

CHAPTER 32

THE HOLY SPIRIT'S WORK IN CREATION

"And the Spirit of God moved upon the face of the waters."

—Genesis 1:2

Close your eyes. Envision your room as you left it this morning as you headed out to school. How do you "see" it?

Are the bedclothes rumpled and dragging onto the floor on one side? Are your dirty socks from the last three days strewn across the floor? Is the wastepaper basket overflowing with paper wads and apple cores and candy wrappers? Are the drawers of your dresser standing open? Are your clothes hung neatly on their hangers, or are they thrown across the back of a chair or at the foot of the bed (or under it)? As you envision your room as you left it, do you see order or chaos?

God is a God of order. In contrast to how your bedroom might look, God's nature is perfect in its orderliness. Even the seeming disorderly aspects of nature—sudden earthquakes, tornadoes, volcanic eruptions, and other uncontrollable natural disasters—are actually part of the orderliness of God's creation. They are the "pressure valves" that He wisely built into our earth to prevent true chaos!

According to Scripture, one role that the Holy Spirit played in creation was the bringing of order to His creation. Everything in creation—from the precise mixture of elements that we call air to the built–in pressure–

release valves—points to His orderliness. It all has purpose and meaning and significance. And part of God's commission to man in the Garden of Eden (i.e., to have dominion over creation and to subdue it) was the necessity of his learning about, understanding, and respecting that order.

But the Holy Spirit did more than give order to creation. Let's look in this lesson at the many other tasks that He performed in relation to Creation.

Notes from the Teacher's Lesson

The Work of The Holy Spirit in Creation		
Function	Stated	Significance
Life		
Order		
Adornment		
Renewing		

Student Work

The teacher's lesson dealt with the Holy Spirit's work in creation. The following student outline deals with two additional works of the Holy Spirit: His relationship to man in the Old Testament and revelation and inspiration.

Man in the Old Testament

The work of the Holy Spirit in relation to man in the Old Testament is not identical to that which He does for man today. The Holy Spirit was present in Old Testament times, of course, but with certain distinct differences from how He worked later. At Pentecost, however, the Holy Spirit came to take up His *residence* in all believers.

Selective Indwelling

In Old Testament times, the Holy Spirit did not indwell *all* of God's people! Look up the following references that indicate that His indwelling was selective. In each case, name the person He indwelt.

In *Certain* People

- Genesis 41:38— _____
- Daniel 4:8— _____
- Numbers 27:18— _____

Came *Upon* Many

- 1 Samuel 16:13— _____
- Judges 3:10— _____
- Judges 6:34— _____

The ministry of the Holy Spirit in Old Testament times was clearly one of being *with* men and not generally one of being *in* all believers, as in the New Testament following the Day of Pentecost.

Enablement for Service

In Old Testament times, the Holy Spirit gave special enduement (ability) for service in certain situations. Read the following verses and fill in the related blanks as appropriate to show how they indicate this truth and which people were involved.

- Exodus 31:3—_____

  The Holy Spirit gave this man special ability to do what work? (see also Exo. 36:1) _____

  _____

- Judges 14:6—_____

  The Holy Spirit gave him what special enduement? _____

  _____

Restraint from Sin

One of the clear ministries of the Holy Spirit in Old Testament man was that of restraining sin. His very names must have had this effect on men as they considered Him.

Match the following names in the left–hand column with the appropriate references that prove this point in the right–hand column.

	Matthew 3:11–12	A. Spirit of grace
	Romans 8:2	B. Spirit of burning
	Hebrews 10:29	C. Spirit of truth
	John 14:17	D. Spirit of life

Revelation and Inspiration

Definitions

Revelation—the disclosure of that which was previously unknown. Revelation concerns the *material* (i.e., *what* was given).

Inspiration – God's superintending of human authors so that, using their own individual personalities, they composed and recorded without error His revelation to man. Inspiration concerns the *manner* (*how* it was given).

Authorship

The Author of revelation (what) and inspiration (how) is the Holy Spirit.

Match the following phrases in the left–hand column with the correct references that prove this point in the right–hand column.

	Acts 1:16	A. "Holy men of God spake as they were moved by the Holy Spirit"
	2 Timothy 3:16	B. "The Spirit of the Lord spake by me"
	2 Samuel 23:2	C. "Well spake the Holy Ghost by Esaias the prophet"
	Acts 28:25	D. "All scripture is given by inspiration"
	2 Peter 1:21	E. "This scripture must needs have been fulfilled"

Means

The Holy Spirit used several means to accomplish His work of revelation and inspiration.

Look up the following references and write in the blanks the means used in each particular instance.

- Exodus 19:9—_____
- Genesis 20:6—_____
- Isaiah 1:1—_____
- John 1:14—_____

Today, we have the written Word. And we can rest assured that *all* of God's Word has been both revealed and inspired by the Holy Spirit. The Bible has been finished and cannot have anything added to it or anything taken from it.

Note the following facts about God's Word.

- The Bible has been said to contain light to direct you, food to support you, and comfort to cheer you.

- In it paradise is restored, heaven is opened, and the gates of hell are closed.

- Its doctrines are holy, its precepts are binding, its histories are true, and its decisions are immutable.

- It's the traveler's rod, the pilgrim's staff, the pilot's compass, the soldier's sword, and the Christian's character.

- It is a mine of wealth, a paradise of glory, and a river of pleasure.

- It is the light of our understanding, the joy of our hearts, the fullness of our hopes, the clarifier of our affections, the mirror of our thoughts, the consoler of our sorrows, and the guide of our souls through the gloomy labyrinth of time.

  This is the greatest book on earth,
  Unparalleled it stands;
  Its author God, its truths Divine
  Inspired in every word and line,
  Tho' writ by human hands.

Application Activities

1. Using *Nave's Topical Bible* (or a similar reference), read every verse that deals with the *work of the Holy Spirit in creation*. List everything those verses tell about His work in that task.

2. Read and outline chapter 6 ("The Work of the Holy Spirit") and chapter 7 ("The Baptism With the Holy Spirit") of Book III of *What the Bible Teaches* by R. A. Torrey. (Bibliographic data are given in the Recommended Reading List.)

3. Research the eruption of Mount St. Helens in the early 1980s. How did this seemingly chaotic "disaster" actually benefit the region and its flora and fauna? How can we see the orderliness of God's creation in this event?

4. Read and summarize pages 52–55 of *Fundamentals of Faith* by Dr. Bob Jones, Jr. (Bibliographic data are given in the Recommended Reading List.)

5. We have God's Word today because of the work of the Holy Spirit. In the following blank table, list at least four probabilities that would be true if the Holy Spirit had not revealed the Word and four probabilities that would be true had He not inspired it.

What if...	
The Spirit had not revealed the Word?	The Spirit had not inspired the Word?

6. Conduct a study of the doctrine of the inspiration of the Bible. Share your findings with the class, either orally or in a written report. Be sure to explain the significance and importance of this doctrine to practical Christian living.

7. Read one (or more) of the following books on prayer. Look for specific references to the work of the Holy Spirit in the exercise of prayer. (Bibliographic data are given in the Recommended Reading List.)

With Christ in the School of Prayer by Andrew Murray
Power Through Prayer by E. M. Bounds
How to Pray by R. A. Torrey
The Life of Prayer by A. B. Simpson
Too Busy NOT to Pray by Bill Hybels

CHAPTER 33

THE HOLY SPIRIT'S WORK IN SALVATION

"Though Christ merits grace for us, it is the Holy Ghost that works it in us. Though Christ makes the purchase, it is the Holy Ghost that makes the assurance, and seals us to the day of redemption."

—Thomas Watson, *A Body of Divinity*

Mrs. Jameson glanced down the row of students suspiciously. The students were taking an English test, and although she could hardly believe her own eyes, she thought that she had just seen Randy, one of her senior boys, cheating. She quietly walked across the front of the room and down the center aisle between the rows of students, glancing to her right and left slowly and sometimes pausing briefly to answer a student's question or to remind a student to keep his or her work covered.

As she arrived at the back of the room and turned around, she noticed Randy glance surreptitiously over his shoulder in her direction. Satisfied that she was going up a row on the other side of the class and was not looking in his direction, he quickly looked inside the slit on the left arm of his shirt, just above where the cuff buttoned. Then he wrote an answer on his paper. Again he glanced in the direction of Mrs. Jameson, looked inside the slit of his shirt, and wrote down another answer.

After watching this activity for about ten minutes, Mrs. Jameson walked slowly down the row of desks in which Randy was sitting. She stopped at Randy's desk, bent over his shoulder, just as she had done so often when answering other students' questions, and whispered, "May I see what you have in your shirt sleeve?"

Startled, Randy began to stammer that he had nothing in his sleeve. But Mrs. Jameson didn't wait to hear his protest. She slipped her thumb and index finger into the slit of his shirt and withdrew a two–by–three–inch piece of paper. She stood erect and read the words on the paper. They were the answers to some of the most difficult questions on the test!

"See me immediately after class," she whispered sternly as she took Randy's test paper and returned to the front of the room.

Randy's face burned as he watched her back as she strode to the front of the classroom. How he hated her! She had caught him cheating, and he knew what the consequences would be. He would get an *F* on that test, Mrs. Jameson would report him to the principal, Mr. Colby would call his parents, and he wouldn't be eligible to play in the big game on Friday afternoon. And those were just the consequences meted out by the school. No telling what terrible things would happen to him at home after his parents learned of his cheating!

After class, he dutifully reported to Mrs. Jameson's desk. He tried to look contrite. "I can explain that paper, Mrs. Jameson," he began hastily. "You see, I had to work late last night because my dad was sick and couldn't get all of his shelves stocked. I was just trying to help him out, but I didn't have time to study for your test. And I just thought that one or two key words might jog my memory and help me remember the answers. I didn't mean it to look like cheating. Honest. And it's really not cheating anyway because…."

Mrs. Jameson held up her hand, interrupting him. "Don't say anything else, Randy, because you're just digging yourself a deeper hole. You were cheating—pure and simple. What was written on that piece of paper was no memory–jogger; it was answers to specific questions—in fact, the very questions you weren't able to answer in class yesterday and the questions you missed on the quiz a few days earlier."

Randy continued to justify his actions, but each time Mrs. Jameson interrupted him, bringing him back to the fact that what he had done was cheating—"pure and simple." Finally, she paused and looked at him. Her eyes were filled with obvious disappointment.

He saw his chance. He let his lower lip begin to quiver, ever so slightly at first but then increasingly. He managed to manufacture a little saltwater in one eye and coax it to trickle down his cheek by lowering his head suddenly. He dramatically brushed it aside and said in a hushed voice, "I'm sorry, Mrs. Jameson. I don't know why I gave into such a temptation. I'm so ashamed of myself. It'll never happen again, I promise." He glanced up to see if the teacher was buying his performance.

"Randy, if this were the first time you had cheated, I might believe you. In fact, I *do* believe that you're sorry." Randy's heart jumped. Maybe she was buying it after all! But then she continued, "I believe that you're sorry—sorry that you got caught! If you were truly sorry all of the other times you've told me you were sorry, you wouldn't let it happen. You wouldn't be making provision for cheating. You're sorry but only that you got caught and will have to suffer the consequences of your behavior. You're not sorry over your sin."

She reminded him of the inevitable consequences of cheating—as if she needed to tell him again—and then dismissed him and began filling out the Discipline Referral Slip that she would take to the office at the end of the day. Randy stomped out of the room, muttering under his breath and slamming the door behind him.. He was angry. Angry that he had gotten caught—how could he have been so careless—but also angry because he knew that Mrs. Jameson was right. She was *always* right!

Just as Randy thought that his "manufactured sorrow" would sway Mrs. Jameson's reaction to his cheating, many people think that just because the Holy Spirit has convicted them of sin and they've said they were sorry and have even walked an aisle and shed some tears they are born again. But they aren't. And that's why they end up returning to their sins.

In this lesson, we discuss the role the Holy Spirit plays in the salvation experience. He convicts sinners of their sin, for sure, but to be truly saved they must have a godly sorrow unto repentance. But the Holy Spirit does much more than convict. He also regenerates, indwells, baptizes, and seals all true believers.

Having looked at the work of the Holy Spirit in the Old Testament, we now turn our attention to His work today. This lesson focuses on the work of the Spirit in salvation. The next lesson will look at His work in the Christian's sanctification and growth.

Notes from the Teacher's Lesson

Conviction of the Holy Spirit

Conviction Defined

- The bringing of a soul to _____ _____ so as to be _____, over his_____ over his need of Christ's _____ , and over his impending_____.

Conviction Stated

- _____

The Significance of Conviction

1. Behold: Conviction comes by a _____ of God's _____. It is the responsibility of all who witness to bring a sinner_____ to _____ with the _____ and _____ of God.

2. Broken: True conviction can be detected by a _____ and humiliated _____ over one's _____ condition.

The Regeneration and Indwelling of the Holy Spirit

Regeneration and Indwelling Defined

- Regeneration: God's supernatural act of imparting_____ _____ to those who believe in Christ.

- Indwelling: The Holy Spirit _____ inside _____ believer, regardless of his spiritual condition.

Regeneration and Indwelling Stated

- Regeneration: _____

- Indwelling: _____

The Significance of Regeneration and Indwelling

- Regneration:

  1. _____

  2. _____

- Indwelling:

  1. _____

  2. _____

The Baptizing of the Holy Spirit

Baptism Defined

- That act of the Holy Spirit whereby He _____ a believer _____ into the _____ of _____ .

  1. _____

  2. _____

  3. _____

  4. _____

Baptism Stated

- _____

The Significance of Spirit Baptism

1. _____
2. _____
3. _____

The Sealing of the Holy Spirit

Sealing Defined

- That act of the Holy Spirit whereby He places His _____
  _____ of _____
  upon us and shuts us up to _____ .

Sealing Stated

- _____

The Significance of Sealing

1. _____
2. _____
3. _____

Application Activities

1. Focus on the Holy Spirit in the Word. Read Acts 4–5, and record all that you learn concerning the Holy Spirit in these chapters.

2. Focus on the Holy Spirit in His providences. Record your salvation experience, showing how the Holy Spirit _drew_ you to Christ in each of the following of His activities:

- How you were *convicted* of your sin and how you know that your conviction was truly brought about by the Holy Spirit
- How the Holy Spirit *regenerated* you (the transformation that took place in your life when you got saved)
- How you are sure that He *indwells* you
- How He has proved to you that you have been *baptized* into Christ (i.e., that He cares for you since you are now bone of His bone and flesh of His flesh)
- How His *sealing* (ownership, authority, and security) has affected your life

3. Using *Nave's Topical Bible* (or a similar reference), read every verse that deals with the *work of the Holy Spirit in salvation*. List everything those verses tell about His work in that task.

4. Explain why mere conviction of sin is not a guarantee of salvation. Similarly, explain why being sorry is not enough for salvation.

CHAPTER 34

THE HOLY SPIRIT'S MINISTRY TO BELIEVERS

"I cannot live the Christian life by making up my mind I am going to live that life. I cannot live the Christian life by any fleshly activity or mental cleverness. I must have, and be filled with, this Holy Spirit. Our churches can do nothing which is really effective for the Kingdom of God without the Spirit."

—G. Campbell Morgan, "The Mediating Ministry of the Holy Spirit,"
The Best of G. Campbell Morgan

How often we are guilty of rushing ahead with *our* plans without first seeking God's counsel or of trying to do *God's* work using *our* methods!

On the individual level, for example, we know that spiritual success comes only to those who are meditating in God's Word and obeying what He reveals to them therein. But we so often are "too busy" doing God's work that we "don't have time" to pray and seek His face or to read His Word and listen to His voice speaking to us through it.

And on the corporate level, we know that God teaches that His work in the church is to be financed through the giving of tithes and offerings of His people. Yet, so often churches use a variety of other fund-raising schemes—from borrowing at exorbitant interest rates to conducting bake sales and selling raffle tickets—to fund their ministries. Whenever He commands us to live by faith in His ability to provide for our every need, we often lag behind His expectations and live only by sight because of our unbelief.

As G. Campbell Morgan said, whether individually or as the Church of God, we cannot succeed on sheer willpower or determination. When we do things based on self–determination and self–empowerment, we distrust and displease God and end up falling back into unbelief.

Rather, we must have the empowerment of the Holy Spirit. The Holy Spirit is called "the Comforter," but He doesn't sing us a lullaby; He makes us strong. He is also called *paraclete*, someone who walks along beside, but He doesn't simply put His arm around our shoulders and commiserate with us; He acts as our divine attorney, pleading our case before the Father.

The Holy Spirit guides us into all truth and teaches, empowers, and equips us for God's service. Once we come to realize the true extent of His work on our behalf, we will be less likely to try doing things *our* way, especially when we're trying to do *God's* work. Rather, we'll be suppliant, seeking His assistance and instruction and living by faith as His dutiful servants.

This lesson concludes our study of the blessed Trinity of the Godhead. We trust that it has only whetted your appetite to continue looking more deeply into the blessed God and Savior, the Lord Jesus Christ. The glorious fact is that there will never be a day when you cannot meet with Him. There will never be an hour so dark that you cannot see Him. There will never be a problem so great as to obscure a glorious view of your God. And this is true because of the ministry of the Holy Spirit!

God's Word is meaningless apart from the Holy Spirit. Without the illuminating power of the Spirit, we could read the Word all day and never see Him. Thus, as glorious as the Father is and as wonderful as our Savior is, they cannot be known or enjoyed apart from the Holy Spirit.

This final lesson on the Holy Spirit focuses on this important aspect of the Spirit's ministry.

Notes from the Teacher's Lesson

Responsibilities in the Spiritual Growth Process (2 Cor. 3:18)

Our Responsibility: _____

_____

_____

The Holy Spirit's Responsibility: _____

_____

_____

DeadMan=	BODY	SOUL

Lost Man=	BODY	SOUL	SPIRIT *EMPTY*

Saved Man=	BODY	SOUL	SPIRIT HOLY SPIRIT

CARNAL ... SPIRITUAL

BODY	SOUL	SPIRIT

Spirit

- _____

- _____

- _____

- _____

- _____

Although man is a tripartite being, not all of those parts may be operating efficiently at the same time. For example, the body's senses may be dulled; hence, the body feeds the soul insufficient information on which to make proper decisions. (A blind man or a deaf man might be good examples of this problem.)

Similarly, man's spirit might be the following:

1. Absent
2. Inoperative
3. Subservient

As a result, the soul is robbed of sufficient data for making proper decisions.

If a man has no spirit (it is absent), he is dead physically. All human beings have a spirit.

If a man doesn't have the Holy Spirit, he is dead spiritually. The Holy Spirit within makes a person alive spiritually. (Read Rom. 8:9 and Eph. 2:1.)

Although unsaved men have a spirit, their spirits are inoperative apart from the Holy Spirit. God made man's spirit to operate only when it is united with God's Spirit.

If the Holy Spirit indwells a man's spirit, the man is saved. Note that the Holy Spirit does not indwell man's soul but his spirit. From there, He sets up headquarters to gain control of the soul.

If man's body is dominant over the spirit and his spirit is subservient to the body, the man is carnal (i.e., fleshly).

If man's spirit, in conjunction with the Holy Spirit, is dominant over the body and in control of the soul, the man is spiritual.

Soul

- Mind:_____
- Will:_____
- Emotions:_____

Body

- _____
- _____

- _____
- _____
- _____

Being Mighty in Spirit (Eph. 3:16)

That He would grant you, according to the riches of His glory, to be strengthened with might by His spirit in the inner man.

1. Ensure that the _____ is within (Rom. 8:9).

2. _____on the_____ through meditation (Rom. 12:2).

3. _____ with the _____ (1 Thess. 5:19).

4. Make no _____ for the _____ (Rom. 13:14).

Student Work

Other Ministries of the Holy Spirit

The teacher's lesson dealt with the work of the Spirit in helping us discern and make spiritual choices. But the Spirit ministers to believers in yet other ways, too. Consider, for example, the following points.

He Gives Gifts

A spiritual gift is a God–given ability for service. According to 1 Corinthians 12:8–11, how is it given? It is given _____ _____ Who gives to every man _____ as He _____. Hence, we learn…

- *What* the gifts are
- *How* they are given
- What *kinds* of gifts are given

Read Romans 12:6–8; 1 Corinthians 12:8–10, 28–30; and Ephesians 4:11. Then list all of the various gifts mentioned in these verses. (Note: some gifts are mentioned in every passage, but you need to list each gift only once.)

- Romans 12:6–8— _____
  _____

- 1 Corinthians 12:8–10— _____
  _____
  _____

- 1 Corinthians 12:28–30—_____

- Ephesians 4:11— _____

Because the Holy Spirit gives these abilities as He desires, the practice of praying for special gifts is unscriptural. It is, however, our responsibility to *discover* which gifts we possess and to *develop* them to their fullest extent and use.

Some of these gifts, including the gift of tongues, are *not* given today. First Corinthians 13:8 makes plain that *tongues was not a permanent gift*. A study of 1 Corinthians 14 also makes clear that *tongues was a special gift for the early church, given as a sign to the unbelieving Jew that God had turned His back on the Jews and that the gospel was now for the Gentiles*. Once this sign had been clearly observed and witnessed by the Jews, it was no longer needed; therefore, it was dropped.

He Fills

Record and memorize Ephesians 5:18. _____
_____
_____

What It Means to Be Filled

The filling of the Spirit can be understood when we compare it with a man who is drunk from having consumed wine or other alcoholic beverage. The central point of the filling of the Spirit is *control*. Just as a man who is drunk with wine is *under the control of* the beverage, a man who is filled with the Spirit is *controlled by* the Spirit.

Why We Should Be Filled

Note that Ephesians 5:18 is a command. That alone is reason enough to desire His filling. Believers—without exception—are expected to be filled. The filling of the Spirit is not something for only a select few; it is a *requirement* for *every* Christian.

How Often a Christian Must Be Filled

Is the filling of the Spirit a once–for–all experience, or must it be repeated periodically? The answer to this question is found in Ephesians 5:18. The verb *be filled* is in the present tense, indicating that the experience is a repeated experience. The verse is actually saying, "*Keep on being filled.*"

This fact is illustrated in the experience of the apostles. They were filled on the Day of Pentecost (see Acts 2:4), and a short time later, they were filled again (see Acts 4:31). The important point to remember is that their need to be filled the second time was not because some sin had come into their lives and they had "lost" their original filling. Rather, they needed His control *in a new area* of their lives. In other words, repeated fillings may be necessary because, as Charles Ryrie wrote in *A Survey of Bible Doctrine*, "new areas of life come to light which need to be brought under the control of the Spirit." Of course, we also need to be refilled each time sin or our ego takes control away from the Spirit.

Conditions for Being Filled

How does one get filled with the Spirit? Does it come by agonizing prayer? Ryrie suggests that there are three conditions for the filling of the Spirit.

- *There must be a dedication of self to God for His use and control.* Because the filling involves control, self must be dethroned and God enthroned through an act of dedication. However, just walking forward during a church service and making an initial decision to dedicate yourself to the Lord is insufficient. There must be *continual* dedication of self to Him. It is a daily dedication.

- *We must not grieve the Spirit* (see Eph. 4:30). We have already discussed this point in an earlier lesson. What two areas grieve the Spirit? _____ .

- *We must depend on the Holy Spirit* (see Gal. 5:16). Walking is itself an act of dependence. When one foot is lifted, the body depends on the other foot for support. Progress can be made only by trusting. So it is in the Christian life. To be Spirit–filled is to be Spirit–dependent. We walk in absolute faith in His power and presence.

Results of Being Spirit–Filled

The following four characteristics accompany a Spirit–filled person.

- *Christlikeness.* Galatians 5:22 lists the nine–fold fruit of the Spirit. List them.

  _____

  _____

  _____

  _____

- *Worship and praise.* Ephesians 5:18 is followed by verses 19–20, which indicate that a person who is Spirit–filled will do two things associated with worship— _____ _____. (Do you have these characteristics?)

- *Submissiveness.* Ephesians 5:21 makes this point clear. According to this verse, to whom do we submit? _____ _____ Therefore, when He is in control, there is harmony and unity with our friends, our parents, and even our enemies! When self is in control, however, there are jealousies, envyings, criticisms, and cliques.

- *Boldness.* Spirit–filling will result in people sharing the gospel of Christ and in souls being saved. In every instance in the New Testament when the filling of the Spirit was mentioned, it was accompanied by the use of the tongue in proclaiming the gospel in boldness.

Do you have these marks? Are you filled with the Spirit? Why not confess the sins that grieve Him and dedicate yourself to Him right now?

He Teaches

According to John 16:12–15, what is the content of the Spirit's teaching?

_____

How does the Spirit teach believers? As a believer studies the Word and listens to other believers teach the Word, the Spirit illuminates (enlightens) the person's heart and gives meaning to and understanding of what is being taught. This is one sign that a person is saved! If one can never seem to grasp the Word and it doesn't make sense, or if his or her heart does not hunger to know the Word, the person must not be born again.

He Guides

One who walks in close fellowship with the Lord will detect the very heart–desire of the Spirit (see Rom. 8:14). He urges and leads in God's will very softly and His guiding hand moves but slightly so that we will give more careful attention to Him. But because His way is soft, we have to be very quiet and keep our eyes fastened intently on Him if we would know His will.

He Gives Assurance

The Holy Spirit indwells every believer to tell him that he is saved (Rom. 8:16; 1 John 3:24; 4:13). A person who doubts his salvation is one of the following:

- Not saved
- Not listening
- Calling the Holy Spirit a liar (which a saved person will not do)

He Helps Us in Our Prayers

The Spirit is involved in our praying in two ways. First, He guides and directs us as we pray so that we bring to God those things that are in His will (Eph. 6:19). Second, He utters our true heart feelings to God when we are unable to express what we need or want to say (Rom. 8:26).

Application Activities

1. Focus on Him in the Word. Read Acts 6 and 8 and record the way the Holy Spirit gave gifts, filled, empowered, taught, led or guided, gave assurance, or answered prayers in these verses.

2. Focus on Him in providences. Record a providence (any category) in which the Holy Spirit definitely led or guided in a particular situation.

3. Record a providence in which the Holy Spirit comforted you in a time of need and/or interceded for you when you either did not know how to pray or were so distraught that you could only offer sighs and He interceded "with groanings which cannot be uttered."

4. If you have not already done so, read and outline chapter 6 ("The Work of the Holy Spirit") and chapter 7 ("The Baptism With the Holy Spirit") of Book III of *What the Bible Teaches* by R. A. Torrey. (Bibliographic data are given in the Recommended Reading List.)

5. Using *Nave's Topical Bible* (or a similar reference), read every verse that deals with the *ministry of the Holy Spirit to believers*. List everything those verses tell us about His work in that task.

6. Research and write a short paper showing that "speaking in tongues" is no longer an operative gift of the Spirit.

CHAPTER 35

THE FIRST—CLAIM PRINCIPLE

"If the Spirit takes charge of your life, He will expect unquestioning obedience in everything. He will not tolerate in you the self–sins [self–love, self–pity, self–seeking, self–confidence, self–righteousness, self–aggrandizement, and self–defense] even though they are permitted and excused by most Christians."

—A. W. Tozer, "The Divine Conquest," *A Treasury of A. W. Tozer*

During our studies this year, we frequently referred to the facts of God's omniscience and providence—God knows everything, and He works out every detail of our lives such that they bring about His glory and our ultimate good. Perhaps we admit these facts and even claim to base our lives on them. But how often our actions belie our *true* beliefs: *we think that we know better than God what is best for us!*

God's Word tells us that the way up is down, but we want to "climb the ladder of success." He tells us that the way to positions of leadership is through servanthood, but we all seem to want to tell everyone else what to do. He teaches that "before honor is humility," but we follow man's way of self–promotion. And the results of our self–absorption and self–centeredness? Self–deception and self–defeat, the very opposite of what we intend for ourselves! How much better if we would simply take God at His Word, obey His principles, and give Him first place in every decision we must make.

This is the topic with which we end our study this year. Pay very close attention during the teacher's lesson. This lesson is without question the most important lesson you'll receive in this class this year!

Notes from the Teacher's Lesson

The First–Claim Principle Stated:

The _____ principle (Matt. 6:33)

The _____ of the principle

_____ He is—

- _____ (Rom. 14:7–11)

- _____ of the _____ (Eph. 1:22–23)

- _____ (Col. 1:15–18)

_____ He has_____ for us (Phil. 2:5–11)

_____ He is to us (1 Cor. 6:19–20)

The _____ of the principle:

C _____ (Ps. 31:15; Luke 9:57–62)

L _____ (Matt. 6:33)

A _____ (Col. 3:2; 2 Cor. 8:5)

I _____ (Prov. 3:9)

M_____ (2 Cor 10:5; Rom. 12:1)

Application Activities

1. Make a chart showing how the First–Claim Principle applies in each of the listed areas of your life. (Give both the references and a short synopsis of how the principle applies to each area named.)

The Broad Applicability of the First–Claim Principle		
Area of Life	References	Practical Applications
Everyday activities and involvements		
Choice of college		
Choice of a major/minor		
Dating relationships		
Choice of a mate		
Choice of a specific job		
Financial planning		
Family planning		
Child–rearing methods		
Vacation planning		
Community services/ involvements		
Political involvements		
Music		
Art		
Literature		
Visual media		
Personal health, safety, and well being		
Other areas of your personal life		

2. Read and write a two–page summary of the key principles discussed in *The Power of Commitment* by Jerry White. (Bibliographic data are given in the Recommended Reading List.)

3. Read and report (either orally or in writing) on *The 24–Hour Christian* by Earl Palmer. (Bibliographic data are given in the Recommended Reading List.)

4. Interview someone whose Christian testimony and ministry you admire. (This person may or may not be in "full–time Christian service." He or she might have a "secular" job but still be an exceptional witness on the job, in the community, or in the church.) Ask this person about, among other things, how the Holy Spirit directed him into his particular ministry and how the First–Claim Principle applies to his daily life.

5. Read and summarize the truths found in chapter 3 ("Right Thinking About the Spirit–Filled Life") of Bill Hull's book *Right Thinking*. How can you apply those truths to your life today?

6. Many people ignore the First–Claim Principle, emphasizing "all these things" in life rather than "seek ye first the kingdom of God." Read and report on one of the following books that present the dangers and vanity of such an unbiblical approach to life.

   • *How to Balance Competing Time Demands* by Doug Sherman and William Hendricks
   • *Total Life Management* by Bob Shank
   • *Perilous Pursuits: Our Obsession with Significance* by Joseph M. Stowell
   • *More to Life than Having it All* by Bob Welch
   • *The Rest of Success* by Denis Haack
   • *Let God Help You Choose: Making Decisions that Matter* by Roger C. Palms
   • *The Secrets of Deciding Wisely* by Ron Kincaid

7. Read the biography of someone whose life exemplified the application of the First–Claim Principle.

8. Conduct an in–class debate over the lesson's assertion that every Christian student should plan to attend a Christian college *unless God specifically directs otherwise.*

9. Conduct an in–class debate over the lesson's assertion that every Christian student should pursue a "full–time ministry" *unless God specifically directs otherwise.*

10. For each of the following "secular" occupations, list ways in which a Christian can conduct it as his or her "full–time Christian ministry."

Occupation/Career Field	How to Make It a Full–Time Ministry
Doctor/nurse	
Lawyer/paralegal	
Engineer	
Architect	
Computer programmer	
Writer	
Accountant	
Financial planner	
Insurance agent	
Mathematician	
Product salesperson	
Other	

RECOMMENDED READING LIST

Bounds, E. M. *Power Through Prayer*. Springdale, PA: Whitaker House, 1982.

Byrd, Dennis. *Rise and Walk*. New York: Harper-Collins Publications, Inc., 1993.

Custer, Stewart. *The Stars Speak: Astronomy in the Bible*. Greenville, SC: Bob Jones University Press, 1977.

Dravecky, Dave. *Comeback*. Grand Rapids, MI: Zondervan Publishing Co. and Harper & Row Publishers, 1990.

_____. *When You Can't Come Back*. Grand Rapids, MI: Zondervan Publishing Co. and Harper & Row Publishers, 1992.

_____. *The Worth of a Man*. Grand Rapids, MI: Zondervan Publishing House, 1996.

Gibbon, Edward. *The Decline and Fall of the Roman Empire*. New York: Dell Publishing Co., Inc., 1963.

Haack, Denis. *The Rest of Success: What the World Didn't Tell You About Having it All*. Downers Grove, IL: InterVarsity Press, 1989.

Hull, Bill. *Right Thinking*. Colorado Springs, CO: NavPress, 1985.

Hybels, Bill. *Too Busy NOT to Pray*. Downers Grove, IL: InterVarsity Press, 1988.

Jones, Bob, Jr. *Fundamentals of Faith*. Greenville, SC: Bob Jones University Press, 1964.

Kincaid, Ron. *The Secrets of Deciding Wisely*. Downers Grove, IL: InterVarsity Press, 1994.

Ketcham, Robert T. *Old Testament Pictures of New Testament Truth*. Des Plaines, IL: Regular Baptist Press, 1965.

Laszlo, Marilyn. *Mission Possible*. Wheaton, IL: Tyndale House Publishers, 1998.

Lockyer, Herbert. *All the Men of the Bible*. Grand Rapids, MI: Zondervan Publishing House, 1958.

Mayhue, Richard. *Spiritual Intimacy*. Colorado Springs, CO: SP Publications/Victor Books, 1990.

McCarthy, Kevin W. *The On-Purpose Person*. Colorado Springs, CO: Piñon Press, 1992.

Murray, Andrew. *With Christ in the School of Prayer*. Old Tappan, NJ: Fleming H. Revell Company, 1953.

Nelson, Marion H., M.D. *How to Know God's Will*. Chicago: Moody Press, 1963.

Owen, John. *The Glory of Christ*. Carlisle, PA: The Banner of Truth Trust, 1994.

Palmer, Earl. *The 24-Hour Christian*. Downers Grove, IL: InterVarsity Press, 1987.

Palms, Roger C. *Let God Help You Choose: Making Decisions That Matter*. Minneapolis: Augsburg Fortress, 1989.

Pickering, Ernest. *Biblical Separation: The Struggle for a Pure Church*. Schaumburg, IL: Regular Baptist Press, 1979.

Plumer, William S. *A Treatise on Providence*. Harrisonburg, VA: Sprinkle Publications, 1993.

Shank, Bob. *Total Life Management*. Portland, OR: Multnomah Press, 1990.

Shelley, Percy B. "Ozymandias," in *English Literature*, Donald B. Clark et al., eds. Toronto: The Macmillan Company, 1960 (p. 667).

Sherman, Doug, and William Hendricks. *How to Balance Competing Time Demands*. Colorado Springs, CO: NavPress, 1989.

Simpson, A. B. *The Life of Prayer*. Camp Hill, PA: Christian Publications, 1989.

Smith, Hannah Whitall. *The Christian's Secret of a Happy Life*. Old Tappan, NJ: Fleming H. Revell Company, 1942.

Spurgeon, C. H. *All of Grace*. Springdale, PA: Whitaker House, 1983.

Steidl, Paul M. *The Earth, the Stars, and the Bible*. Phillipsburg, NJ: Presbyterian and Reformed Publishing Company, 1979.

Stowell, Joseph M. *Perilous Pursuits: Our Obsession with Significance*. Chicago: Moody Press, 1994.

Torrey, R. A. *What the Bible Teaches*. Grand Rapids, MI: Baker Book House, 1933.

_____. *How to Pray*. Chicago: Moody Press, n.d.

_____. *How to Succeed in the Christian Life*. Chicago: Moody Press, n.d.

Tozer, A. W. *The Pursuit of God*. Harrisonburg, VA: Christian Publications, Inc., 1948.

Watson, Thomas. *A Body of Divinity*. Carlisle, PA: The Banner of Truth Trust, 1997.

Welch, Bob. *More to Life than Having it All*. Eugene, OR: Harvest House Publishers, 1992.

White, Jerry. *The Power of Commitment*. Colorado Springs, CO: NavPress, 1985.

GLOSSARY

Ascension Christ's visible and bodily departure from earth after His resurrection from the grave and His return to heaven from the Mount of Olives

Atonement The reconciliation of God and man through the death of Jesus Christ

Attributes of God The characteristics of God's essential being; there are two types of attributes: natural and moral

Baptizing by the Holy Spirit The act of the Holy Spirit whereby He places a believer once and for all into the body of Jesus Christ

Being Focusing on the inner qualities of holiness

Conviction The bringing of a soul to behold the Being of God such as to be broken over his sinfulness, over his need of Christ's righteousness, and over his impending judgment

Deity of Christ The doctrine that Jesus Christ is God, the Second Person of the Godhead and both the Jehovah and the Angel of Jehovah of the Old Testament

Divine Love Derived from God

Doing Focusing on right actions: behaving, witnessing, tithing, studying, praying, etc.

Essence of God God's essential being or substance; the reality itself

Eternality The doctrine that God is infinite (without limitation) in existence

First–Claim Principle The doctrine that Jesus Christ has first claim on every aspect of the life of every saved person

God's love That in God which moves Him to give Himself and His gifts spontaneously, voluntarily, and righteously for the good of personal beings regardless of their merit or response

Grace God's giving us what we do not deserve

Holiness The inward progressive work of the Holy Spirit, through Christ, of setting apart the believer to God

Human love Desires based on physical, emotional, mental, and intellectual attractions

Immutability The doctrine that God is unchanging and unchangeable

Impeccability The doctrine that God is not capable of sinning or liable to sin, that He is free from fault or blame

Incarnation Christ's taking on a human body, being born of a woman, and living as a man, yet without sin

Indwelling The Holy Spirit's living permanently inside every believer regardless of his spiritual condition

Knowing Focusing on facts and doctrine

Legalism Judging one's salvation by his or her performance of deeds

Life Message A record of what God has done and is doing in one's life that he or she tells to others

Lust Desires based solely on physical attraction

Meditation Thinking about the knowledge of God, allowing those meditations to permeate one's life, and living upon that knowledge

Mercy God's not giving us what we deserve

Omnipotence The doctrine that God cannot do anything that is absurd or self-

	contradictory but that He is able to do whatever He wills. As such, He is in control and can change the situation whenever He wills.
Omnipresence	The doctrine that God is present everywhere
Omniscience	The doctrine that God knows everything
Prayer	Worship addressed to the Father in the name of the Son in the power of the Holy Spirit
Propitiation	Satisfaction
Providence	God's ordering all issues and events after the counsel of His will to His own glory; the events and circumstances in our lives that, controlled and designed by God, are for our good and God's glory; providences come in two types: mercies and judgments
Reconciliation	The making of peace between opposing parties
Regeneration	God's supernatural act of imparting to those who believe in Christ; to be "born again"
Renewing	The adjustment of the moral and spiritual vision and thinking to the mind of God
Resurrection	The doctrine that Jesus Christ arose literally and bodily from the grave, by the power of God, three days after His crucifixion and showed Himself by "many infallible proofs" to His disciples
Sanctification	The act of setting one apart to God from sin and growing in the grace and knowledge of God
Sealing	The act of the Holy Spirit whereby He places His divine stamp of ownership upon believers and shuts them up to Himself forever
Sentimentalism	Focusing on love as the object and purpose of the Christian life
Trinity	The doctrine that God, though one, is three distinct persons—the Father, the Son, and the Holy Spirit; three eternal distinctions in one divine essence; the Father planned man's salvation, the Son provided salvation, and the Holy Spirit performs salvation.
True Religion	Communion between God and man
Unity of God	The doctrine that there is only one living and true God, who is undivided and indivisible
Worship	The occupation of the heart with a known God